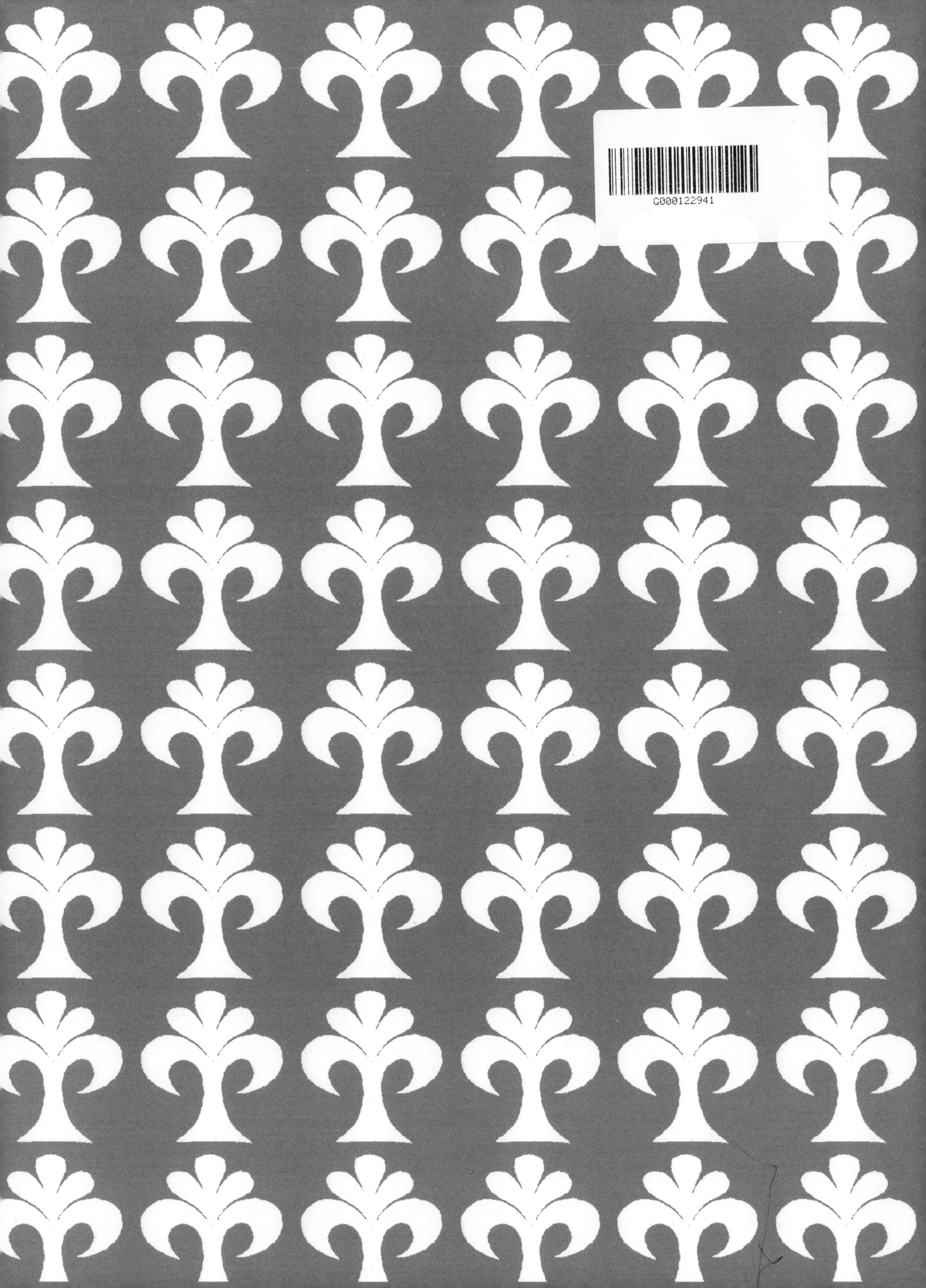
G000122941

Delhi · Agra · Jaipur

Delhi · Agra · Jaipur

The Golden Triangle

Lustre Press

Delhi ◊ Banaras ◊ Agra ◊ Jaipur

First published 1994. M--75, Greater Kailash-II Market, New Delhi-110 048, INDIA, Tel: (011) 6442271, 6462782, 6460886-7. Fax: (011) 6467185.

First published in 1982 by Roli Books International

Original text: *Sumi Krishna Chauhan.* Revised by *Kishore Singh, Suhit K. Sen.*
Walking Through Delhi's History (Pages 40-41) by *Dr. Narayani Gupta.*
Typesetting: Fleming George P. & Monika Raj Malik.

ISBN: 81-7437-062-5

PHOTO CREDITS
Karoki Lewis: Pages 6, 24 (top and bottom), 30, 31, 32, 33, 71, 74-75, 76, 78, 79, 80 (top and bottom), 81 (top and bottom), 82-83, 84, 85, 86, 87 (top and bottom), 88, 89, 92, 93. *D.N. Dube:* Pages 7, 8, 9 10, 11, 12-13, 14 (bottom), 17, 18-19, 20, 23, 25 (bottom), 26-27, 34-35, 36, 37, 42, 43, 45 (bottom), 49, 52 (top and bottom), 65. *Pramod Kapoor:* Cover, pages 14 (top), 38-39, 46-47, 62-63, 66-67, 68, 69, 70, 77, 90-91, 95. *Ashok Dilwali:* Pages 1, 2-3, 44 (top), 50-51, 53 (top and bottom), 54-55, 56-57, 58, 60, 61. *Amit Pasricha:* Pages 15 (top), 16, 25 (top), 28, 29. *Aman Nath & Francis Wacziarg:* Pages 72, 73. *Robyn Beeche:* Page 96. *Rohit Chawla:* Page 48. *Ravi Kaimal:* Page 22. *Aditya Patankar:* Page 94. *Sondeep Shankar:* Page 15 (bottom).

Printed and bound by Star Standard (Pte) Ltd, Singapore

Cover: *Dancer and musicians at Samode's Durbar Hall.* ***Half-title page:*** *Detail from a brilliantly glazed tile at Chini ka Rauza, Agra's riverfront tomb built for Shah Jahan's finance minister, Shukrulla.* ***Title page:*** *A dreamy view of the Taj Mahal.* ***This page:*** *The illuminated Rashtrapati Bhawan and Parliament House, symbolic of India's democratic power.*

DELHI

The Heart of Empire

No city in India has had as long, as continuous and as varied a history as Delhi's. In the last 3,000 years it has seen the rise and fall of great empires, ruled in turn by the Hindus, the Muslims and the British. It has had a taste of the Hun invasions, and it has been plundered and ravaged by Nadir Shah. As the capital of independent India, it has become a political nerve centre. Through the centuries the magic of Delhi has remained unbroken. There is an old song that says: *"Dilli shahr suhana aur kanchan barse neer"* (Delhi city is beautiful, and gold showers down like rain).

The power and the glory of Delhi's pageant of rulers are reflected in the monuments which have survived through the centuries. These monuments stand in the so-called seven cities of Delhi. Over a thousand are listed, not including the ruins which have their own story to tell.

The city of Delhi had acquired its present name before it came under Muslim rule at the turn of the twelfth century. Popular tradition traces the name to Raja Dillu who is said to have ruled here in the first century BC. But historians believe it was christened Dilli by the Rajput rulers who founded the first of the medieval cities of Delhi in the eleventh century.

Dilli was probably the capital of what is now Haryana. The earliest local reference to it is a 1276 inscription in the Palam *baoli* (stepped well), though the name occurred for the first time a century earlier in an inscription near Udaipur in Rajasthan. The Palam *baoli* inscription mentions Yoginipura as an alternative name and also refers to the village of Palamba, clearly the same as the present-day Palam village which is adjacent to the Indira Gandhi International Airport.

Today, Delhi's nine million residents are sprawled across an area of 1,485 sq km on the banks of the river Yamuna, which flows down from a Himalayan glacier to join the mighty Ganga at Allahabad. The city lies in the hot and arid region between the Indus valley and the alluvial Gangetic plain.

Very little of Delhi's original flora and fauna have withstood the pressures of urbanization. The only surviving natural areas are the northern and western ridges. These hilly spurs are the trailing end of the Aravalli range, one of the oldest mountain systems in the world.

The ridge is characterized by a typically arid vegetation. The thorny *babool* and the casuarina with its needle-like leaves are in abundance. A few surviving groups of Rhesus monkeys perch on the bunds of the ridge road. These monkeys are considered sacred by the Hindus. You can also spot an occasional mongoose scurrying through the undergrowth which harbours snakes.

The introduction of planned parks and city forests, and of ornamental trees and plants in the developing areas, has given Delhi its reputation of a garden city. There is always some greenery, even when the temperature soars to over 45° C in summer,

Facing page: *The faithful kneel to pray in the corridors of the Jama Masjid, the country's largest mosque, in the same manner as its founder, Shah Jahan, must have knelt on silken carpets to echo the cries of the faithful — 'There is only one God and Muhammad is His Messenger'. The mosque was completed in 1656, soon after work on the Red Fort had ceased.*

This page: *Detail from a motif behind the throne at Red Fort's Diwan i Am, the hall of public audience. The red sandstone throne was backed by a marble balcony on which the pietra-dura inlay of floral designs and birds (a particular love of Jehangir) echoed Florentine motifs and was perfected under Shah Jahan's guidance.*

The Republic Day Parade marches down New Delhi's most imperial road, Rajpath, on January 26th every year. The procession that starts from Vijay Chowk in front of Rashtrapati Bhawan, marches down towards India Gate, accepting the salute of the nation's President, and winding onwards to culminate at Red Fort. The parade marks the day when the newly independent country accepted the constitution and became a republic.

as sometimes it does, or drops to near freezing point in winter.

The most common trees are the medicinal *neem*, the sacred *peepal* and the fruit-bearing *jamun*. Besides these, a wide variety of flowering trees line the avenues in many parts of the city. They provide shade and a splash of colour in the hot summer months.

The best time to visit Delhi is after the monsoon. From October to February the

weather is pleasant, the cultural season is at its height, the city is bustling with activity, and chrysanthemums and roses and a variety of spring flowers make every roundabout in the city a riot of colour. The Nehru Park, Mahavir Park and the Buddha Jayanti Park are especially attractive. The Mughal Gardens, part of the grounds attached to the Indian President's official residence, the Rashtrapati Bhawan, are open to the public at this time. Laid out in the old Mughal style, these gardens provide a feast of flowers.

Winter is also the best season for birds in the city. A variety of migratory storks, ducks and other waterbirds fly down from Siberia and north Asia. You can see them breeding in many places in and around Delhi. They nest at the Sultanpur lake in Haryana, near Delhi, and at the lake of the Zoological Park in the city itself.

Of the 1,200 species of Indian birds, many can be easily sighted in the city's parks and gardens. Most common are the bulbul and mynah, besides the green bee-eater, the kingfisher, the hoopoe and the black drongo. There are pigeons under the eaves, grey- wattled lapwings, which are said to predict the rain, and the weaver-birds with their beautiful hanging nests.

Before the advent of British rule, Delhi had acquired a synthesis of Hindu and Muslim traditions and a distinct Indo-Islamic culture, rather like that of the city of Lucknow. This was reflected in its crafts, its music and dance, and in its most widely-used language, Urdu. Urdu is a blend of Persian and Khari Boli, the variety of Hindi that was once spoken in the Delhi region and is now another name for Hindi.

After the attainment of independence, the character of Delhi has changed. The thousands of government employees who have come from all over the country have given the capital a bureaucratic stamp. However, they have brought with them their diverse cultures, so that the city has something from every region in India.

The lure of the city draws people from the villages around and the far corners of the country in quest of employment. This puts civic services in the metropolis under increasingly greater pressure and pushes the urban spread in all directions. Delhi is constantly transforming itself — old houses being torn down for new structures, and whole colonies springing up overnight, as it were. Roads are instantly being renamed, to satisfy a new generation, a new ideology. Janpath, which, for instance, means the people's road, was once Queen's Way. For its residents, the streets of Delhi have an age-old charm, eloquently voiced by a Mughal poet who wrote: *"Kahan jain Zauk, Dilli ki gallian chhor kar?"* (Where shall we go Zauk, leaving the streets of Delhi?).

But even today, Delhi is a mixture of the old and the new. Ancient *tongas* (horse carriages) clatter over some of the streets as jets zoom above. Street acrobats, dancing bears and monkeys still provide entertainment in certain parts of the city. At the same time, Delhi offers you the finest talents in Indian classical dance and music. Young jeans-clad men and women stride alongside *purdah*-clad women who, with their faces veiled, walk two paces behind their menfolk in public. This is Delhi, which, its poet-king, Bahadur Shah Zafar, said, was "the jewel of the world where dwelt only the loved ones of fate."

HISTORY

THREE THOUSAND YEARS AGO, THE story goes, Dhritarashtra, father of the one hundred Kauravas, ruled at Hastinapur, on the banks of the river Ganga. To ease the conflict between his sons and the five Pandavas, Dhritarashtra gave his nephews a separate kingdom, Khandavaprastha, on the west bank of the river Yamuna. The Pandavas "measured out a city surrounded by ditches like the sea and provided with high defence walls." This was Indraprastha, according to the story related in the great Hindu epic, the *Mahabharata.*

Indraprastha was a city fit for the gods. "It contained a palace with every luxury; mansions; broad roads and highways, shaded with trees; fountains and squares; and shops filled with rare merchandise. Many citizens and traders from Hastinapur came to reside there, attracted by its beauty and convenience." When the Pandavas defeated their cousins with the aid of Lord Krishna in the epic battle of Kurukshetra, they are said to have returned to Hastinapur, leaving Indraprastha in the care of one of Lord Krishna's kinsmen.

Perhaps this is just a legend. But recent excavations at the site of Purana Qila, the Old Fort, and on the banks of the Yamuna in Delhi, have revealed fine grey earthenware painted in simple black designs. Archaeologists call this Painted Grey Ware and date it to 1000 BC. These settlements belong to the iron and copper ages. The ornaments of this period were beads and bangles made of clay, bone and glass. Houses were made of mud and tools of bone. Significantly, similar finds have been made at many places associated with the story of the *Mahabharata.* Indraprastha is one of these.

The Purana Qila excavations, completed in 1973, revealed earthenware of the Maurya period, *circa* 300 BC. Delhi was part of the vast kingdom of the great Mauryan Emperor Ashoka who embraced Buddhism after he had won a particularly bloody battle at Kalinga, in modern Orissa. Ashoka propagated Buddha's teachings through rock edicts and the well-known Ashokan pillars. A minor rock edict was discovered in 1966 in one of the outcrops near Srinivaspuri, overlooking the Yamuna, not far from the ancient site of Purana Qila. Evidently, Delhi lay on one of the trunk routes of ancient India. Archaeological evidence also suggests that the city was continuously inhabited.

The founding of the first medieval city

A view of Vijay Chowk looking down the imperial eighth city of Delhi with India Gate in the distance and signs of a modern city struggling to find root. It was atop this hill, Raisina, that the foundation stone for the new city was laid at the turn of the century, to be occupied in the '30s when Calcutta was abandoned as the capital. Popular belief has it that the one aim that guided the city's architect was to produce, perhaps centuries later, impressive, imperial ruins!

Though India traces its roots back to thousands of years, and Delhi has had a history as its capital for many of them, yet it reveals few traces of its own culture as a distinctive city. This is probably because as its capital it was ravished, looted and razed several times. Post-independence, it has attracted people from all over the country like the proverbial lodestone, allowing it to grow into a gargantuan metropolis, and in different pockets of the city one now finds traces of the flavours of India such as in the celebration of Durga Puja by the Bengali community.

of Delhi is ascribed to a Rajput chieftain of the Tomara clan. The Tomaras ruled over the rugged Aravalli hills, south of Delhi, in what is now Haryana. They are believed to have first settled in the Surajkund area near Delhi, where they built a large amphitheatre reservoir. This has become a popular picnic spot. A kilometre away, in Anangpur village, there is a dam which had been built by King Anangpal. It was Anangpal who brought the Tomaras 10 km west and built the citadel of Lal Kot in AD 1020. It is on this site that the Qutb Minar now stands.

Lal Kot was captured about a century later by a rival Rajput clan, the Chauhans, who held sway over both Delhi, and Ajmer in Rajasthan. Prithviraj Chauhan, also called Rai Pithora, is one of the most popular figures of Indian history, well known for his valour. He became the ruler in 1170, expanded Lal Kot and added to the temples the Tomaras had built. This extended city was known as Qila Rai Pithora.

Prithviraj was the ruler of Delhi when an Afghan chief, Muhammad Ghuri, overran the Punjab and Sind, and marched towards Delhi. In their first encounter in 1191, Prithviraj was victorious, but with traditional Rajput chivalry he spared Ghuri's life. The following year Ghuri attacked again. Jai Chand, a rival Rajput chieftain, declined to come to Prithviraj's aid; Prithviraj was defeated and killed. This proved to be a turning point in the history of India.

Delhi passed into the hands of a representative of a Ghuri, Qutb-ud-din Aibak, who enthroned himself as Sultan after Ghuri's death in 1206. And thus, Muslim rule in India began. Historians give many causes for the Muslim success. The Rajput kings were divided by personal and political rivalry. Though they were capable of great heroism and individual acts of gallantry, militarily they were inferior to the Muslims. Prithviraj's elephants and infantry, for instance, were no match for Ghuri's 1,20,000 strong cavalry.

When Qutb-ud-din became the Sultan of Delhi in the early thirteenth century, he set about transforming the life and pattern of the city. For the next 600 years, Delhi was to remain under Muslim rule. The impact of Islam would find expression in the city's art and architecture, in its language, poetry and music, even in the customs and traditions of the people.

Even before Qutb-ud-din took over Lal Kot, he had begun destroying the temples built by the Tomaras and Chauhans. He demolished twenty-seven Hindu and Jain temples, and used the materials to build the Quwwat-ul-Islam mosque. In 1209 he began the Qutb Minar, the highest stone tower in India. The tower was completed after Qutb-ud-din's death, by his successor, Iltutmish. At this time there were four Muslim kingdoms in India: Delhi, Bengal, Sind and Lahore. During Iltutmish's war-ridden reign (*circa* 1210-36), the entire territory was united, and power centralized, at Delhi. For this martial success, the king was recognized by the Caliph of Baghdad.

Iltutmish nominated his daughter, Razia, to succeed him. But the elevation of a woman, though sagacious and capable, was not welcomed. Razia ruled briefly and was overthrown by intriguing nobles. Of her successors only Ghiasuddin Balban did the so-called slave dynasty proud. But for the most part the Sultanate remained in a state of confusion. The Khaljis and the Turks contended for supremacy in Delhi, while the Mongols were an ever-present threat on the northern borders. In 1290, the slave dynasty was overthrown by the Khaljis.

The most famous Khalji ruler was the ambitious Ala-ud-din Khalji (1296-1316). He left his stamp on the city of Delhi too. In 1303, he built the circular Alai Fort, or Koshak-i-Siri, "the walls of which were made of stone, brick and lime and which had seven gates." It was this fort at Siri which was demolished by Sher Shah. At this site Sher Shah built a new city near old Delhi, marked today by the Shahbad village. This was the second city of Delhi, but the first original Muslim city. He also dug a vast reservoir for the people of Siri. Today, near its ruins, is a modern residential colony called Hauz Khas, literally 'special reservoir.'

In 1320, the Khalji kingdom was taken over by the Tughlaks, a Turkish tribe. Ghiyas-ud-din Tughlak (1320-25) built himself another capital city, Tughlakabad, 8 km south-east of the Qutb. Tughlakabad was thus the third medieval city of Delhi. Ghiyas-ud-din's son, the crown prince, plotted against him and contrived his death outside Delhi when the Sultan was returning from a battle in Bengal.

One of his successors, Muhammad bin Tughlak (1325-51), was a most extraordinary ruler. Historians have described him variously as madman and genius. One of his most quixotic experiments was an attempt to shift the capital of the Sultanate to a more strategic southern location. He built a new city, Daulatabad, and tried to resettle Delhi's population there. The experiment failed and he resumed ruling from Tughlakabad, though he built yet another city, Jahanpanah, between Qila Rai Pithora and Siri.

The next ruler, Feroz Shah (1351-88), was a man of many parts — scholar and hunter, architect and philanthropist. He planned buildings and irrigation canals from the Sutlej and Yamuna. He repaired old monuments, including the Qutb and Surajkund and built, among other cities, Ferozabad, the fifth city of Delhi. Its large, high-walled citadel, formerly on the banks of the river Yamuna, 3 km upstream of the Purana Qila, is now known as Feroz Shah Kotla. It has lent its name to the famous cricket field which is nearby. He also built several hunting-lodges, one of which lies within the Teenmurti House compound which is now a memorial to India's first Prime Minister, Jawaharlal Nehru. Feroz Shah also built schools, mosques, palaces, bridges, monumental pillars and hospitals.

The rule of the later Tughlaks was marked by confusion and anarchy. As rival princes fought each other in Delhi, the dreaded Timur the Lame set out from Samarqand and reached the Indus in 1398. Devastating all that came in his way, he marched upon Delhi. The terrible Turk routed 10,000 horses, 40,000 infantry and 120 elephants of the Delhi army. He ravaged the city, massacred the people and took thousands of artisans as captives, back to Samarqand. Nothing was left of Delhi but its name. For two months not a bird moved. The city remained in disarray for fourteen years till the Sayyids took over the Sultanate. They were ousted by the Lodis who transferred the capital from Delhi to Agra in 1504. At its height the Lodi kingdom extended from the Punjab to Bihar. But rebellions were always brewing. In this strife-torn period, art and architecture stagnated. The time was ripe for yet another foreign invasion.

"At the time that Machiavelli was collecting materials for *The Prince,*" wrote E. M. Forster, "a robber boy, sorely in need of advice, was scuttling over the highlands of Central Asia. His problem had already engaged the attention and sympathy of the Florentine; there were too many kings about and not enough kingdoms." That young lad was Babar, descended from the mighty Timur and Chinghiz Khan. Babar had failed to overcome Samarqand, and in 1525 he invaded the Punjab. In 1526, on the historic battlefield of Panipat, Babar defeated the Lodi Sultan, occupied Delhi and Agra, and thus laid the foundation of the great Mughal empire in India. His son, Humayun, ruled initially for ten troubled years, unable to consolidate his territory. But during these years he laid the foundations of Dinpanah

Young Sikhs take part in a procession to celebrate the anniversary of one of the ten Gurus or spiritual teachers of the community. The Sikhs come from neighbouring Punjab, are characterised by such distinctive traits as the wearing of unshorn hair under a turban and the carriage of a weapon such as a sword or a dagger, and are known as much for their hard working zeal and zest for life as for their piety.

Overleaf: *An aerial view of the Qutb Minar complex which is seen more for curiosity than for the skilled workmanship of medieval India which led Bishop Heber to describe its magnificent effect thus: 'They built like giants, and they finished like jewellers'. At the centre of this complex is the Minar itself, begun by Qutb ud din Aibak, finished by Iltutmush, modified by Ferozeshah Tughlaq and almost crowned with a cupola by the British. In the foreground is India's first mosque, the Quwwat ul Islam, to one side the Alai Darwaza or gatehouse of Allaudin Khilji, and in a straight line the base of yet another minaret that was never completed, but had it been finished, would have been taller than the Qutb Minar.*

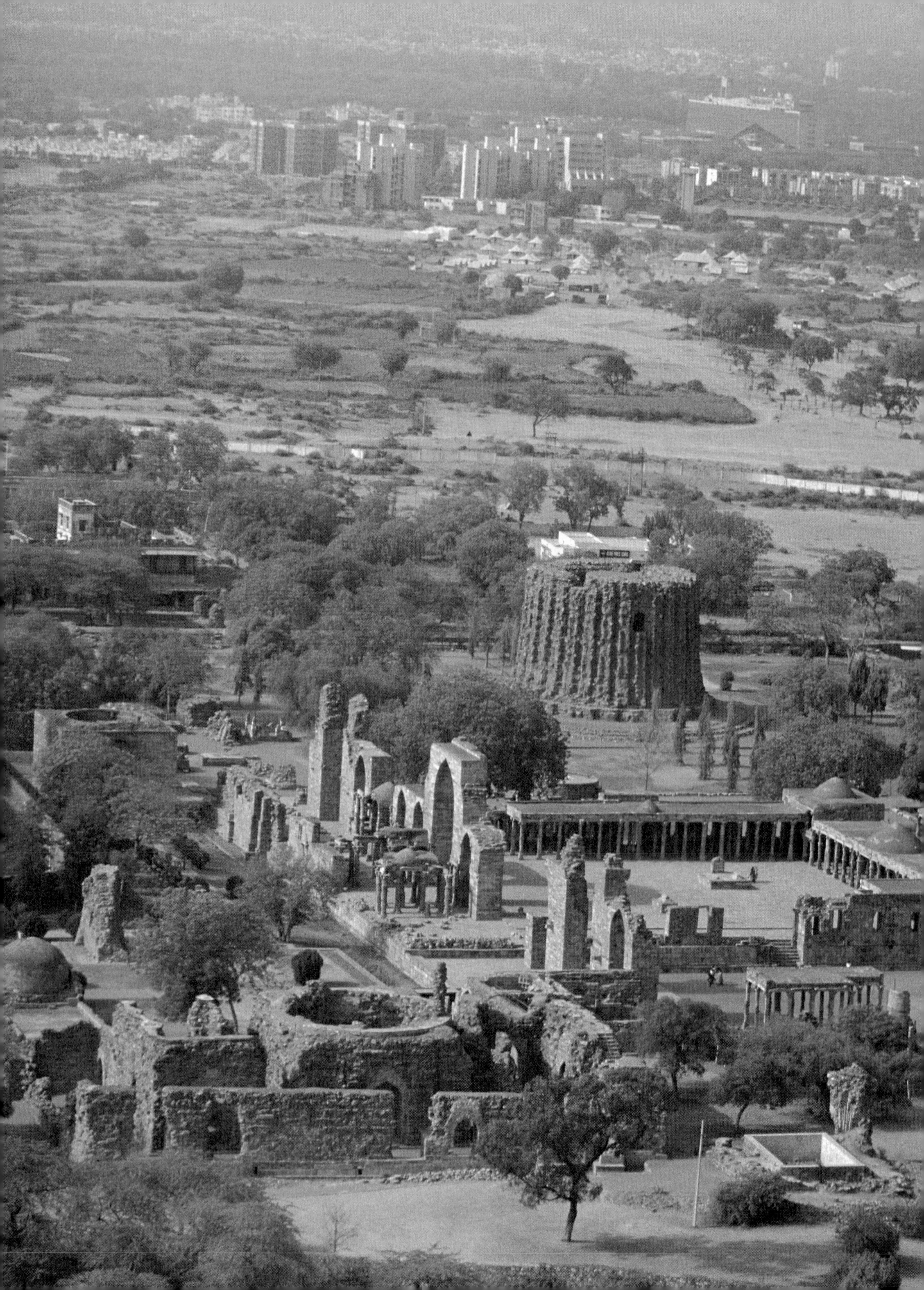

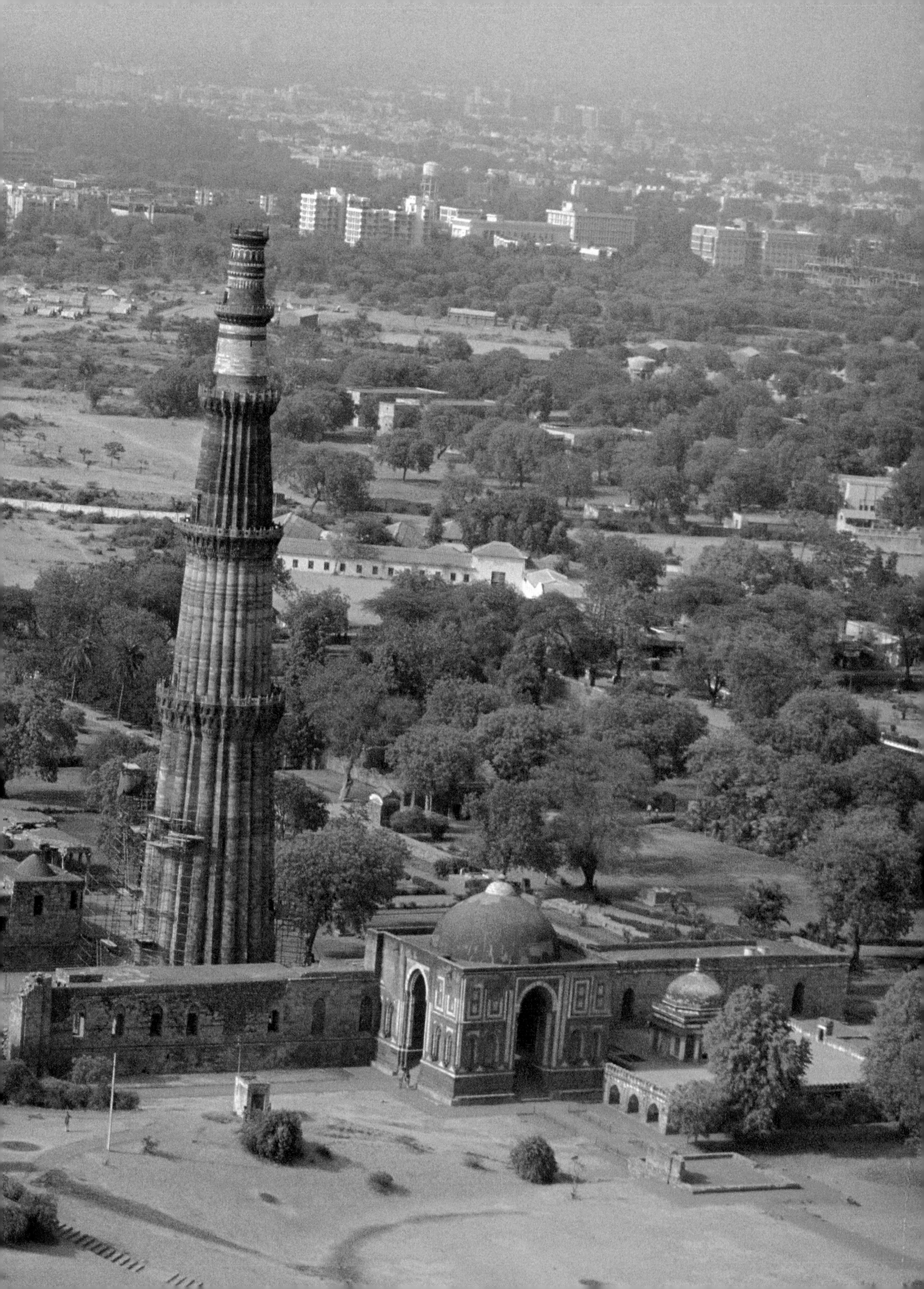

Top: Safdarjung's tomb in Delhi, built for a Lucknawi nobleman by his son, symbolises both the decline of Mughal architecture from its Agra apogee and the turbulence of the period, when Safdarjung fomented civil wars in Delhi under the very nose of the feeble Mughal ruler.
***Above:** The dome of Rashtrapati Bhawan, flanked on either side by the government offices of South and North Block respectively, find reflection in the waters of the pools created in the capital by its architect, Edward Lutyens. This Indo-Saracenic construction is unique combining several elements of north-Indian architecture with studied effect.*

(1533), a new city on the banks of the Yamuna, in the vicinity of the ancient city of Indraprastha.

In 1540, Humayun was ousted by his arch enemy, the Afghan Sher Shah Suri, a scholarly man and an able administrator. Sher Shah laid roads and planted trees, built wells and *sarais* (inns) for travellers and organized the royal post. He laid the original Grand Trunk Road from Lahore down to Delhi and Agra and on towards Dhaka in the eastern reaches of Bengal. On the site of the Pandava capital, Indraprastha, adjacent to Humayun's Dinpanah, which he perhaps first demolished, Sher Shah built the Purana Qila, the sixth medieval city of Delhi. Its ruins still stand on the Delhi-Agra road.

For ten years following Sher Shah's death in 1545, the people of Delhi suffered terribly as rivals struggled for power. There was a severe famine and pestilence. Humayun recovered his throne in 1555 but died shortly after. It is said that his death was caused by a fall down the steep stairs leading to his library in the Purana Qila. Humayun's tomb (built in 1565) in Delhi, one of the gems of Mughal architecture, marks the synthesis of the Persian and Indian traditions which was to flourish in the years to come.

When his father died, Akbar, the greatest of the Mughals, was only thirteen. But during his rule (1556-1605), a happy blend of Hindu and Islamic culture was achieved. This expressed itself in art and life. However, Akbar's story really belongs not to Delhi but to Agra, which was his seat of government. Akbar's son, Jahangir (1605-27), also ruled from Agra, though he sometimes made his headquarters at Lahore, a city that he particularly liked. In Jahangir's time, Delhi was a secondary city ravaged by bubonic plague which took a heavy toll.

The imperial glory of Delhi was restored by Shah Jahan who came to the throne after a struggle, in 1628. Having spent the early years of his reign in Agra (which he made immortal by building the Taj Mahal), Shah Jahan turned his attention to Delhi. He found the congested streets of Agra too narrow for his grand processions and therefore decided to make Delhi the capital in 1638. It took eleven years to build the city of Shahjahanabad — the last of the seven medieval cities of Delhi — with rubble walls, fourteen gates and an imposing citadel, the Lal Qila, or the Red Fort, on the banks of the Yamuna. The polygonal city had housing blocks, parks and bazaars; its marble mosque, the Jama Masjid, was the largest and perhaps most magnificent in India. For almost 350 years, the Walled City of Shahjahanabad, near the ruins of old Ferozabad, has been, and still is, a bustling, living city.

As the mighty Shah Jahan grew old, Delhi was once again gripped by a struggle for power. Aurangzeb imprisoned his ailing father and crowned himself emperor in 1658. He reigned for nearly half a century, during which his expansionist campaigns emptied the treasury, and intellectual and cultural activities declined.

The Mughal empire disintegrated rapidly after Aurangzeb's death in 1707. Delhi suffered under successive monarchs. In

1739, the Persian invader Nadir Shah reduced what was left of the Mughal empire to a wilderness. In a single day, thousands were slaughtered in Shahjahanabad. Nadir Shah spent two months in Delhi and plundered everything of value: the moneychangers' bazaar, the jewellery shops, and the markets were looted; the famous Peacock Throne which Shah Jahan had had installed in the Red Fort, and the invaluable Kohinoor diamond were among his spoils. When he left, he took with him the city's best carpenters, stone cutters, masons, goldsmiths and other craftsmen. Hardly had Shahjahanabad recovered when it was brutally ravished again in 1757 by Ahmad Shah Durrani, a protege of Nadir Shah.

In 1771, the Marathas set Shah Alam II, a descendant of the Mughals, as a puppet king on the throne of Delhi. His authority did not extend beyond the districts of Delhi and Agra. His own people ridiculed him: *"Badshah Shah Alam/Az Dilli ton Palam"* (King Shah Alam/From Delhi to Palam). His ignominy reached its depth when the Rohilla Afghans seized Delhi in 1788, and deposed and blinded him. They occupied the city for over two months, despoiling it till the Marathas reconquered the city.

But in the years of Delhi's decline the history of India was undergoing a radical change. It was the close of the eighteenth century. The British had established themselves along the eastern coast of India as a political power to be reckoned with. Lord Arthur Wellesley was the Governor-General when the Marathas were vanquished in a decisive battle at Delhi by the forces of the British. The puppet Mughal emperor, Shah Alam, came under British protection. The year was 1803.

The peculiar historical conjucture of the middle decades of the nineteenth century presaged an upheaval: this conjuncture was created by the presence of an impoverished north Indian peasantry, a discontented class of landowners, a restive army—and the widespread hankering for the days of Mughal glory. Bahadur Shah Zafar, the nominal Mughal emperor in Delhi, became an emotive symbol which united all discontented groups in an uprising against British rule. In 1857, the whole of north India was convulsed by what is known alternatively as the Sepoy Mutiny, or the First War of Indian Independence.

The rebel troops marched to Delhi and proclaimed the terrified Mughal emperor, Bahadur Shah, as their king. Rebel soldiers from all over the country poured into Delhi and the last vestige of British authority in the city disappeared. The soldiers who could not be paid took to plundering the rich Europeans. A joint Hindu-Muslim proclamation urged all Indians to rise against the alien government. From May to September 1857, the rebels held Delhi, occupying the northern ridge near the British cantonment at Rajpur village, where the University of Delhi now is.

It was only when General John Nicholson came from the Punjab with reinforcements that the Kashmiri Gate was blown up—the very same gate that had been rebuilt by the British after an earthquake in 1720. After the rebels were defeated, British

***Top:** Humayun's Tomb, built in the memory of the emperor by his widow: made of sandstone and marble, and believed to be the finest example of Mughal architecture in Delhi, it has often been labelled a precursor to Agra's Taj Mahal. Humayun's Tomb dwarfs that of his father, Babar who lies buried in one of the smaller tombs within the same complex.*
***Above:** Purana Qila, from where Humayun once held sway over Hindustan, was wrested from him by Sher Shah, only to revert to him again shortly before his own death from a fall down the stairs of the Sher Mandal library within its ramparts.*

An overview of the battlements of Red Fort, the capital of Shah Jahan's Shahjahanabad, with decorative arches and cupolas lending elegance to its sturdy walls. Once emperors ruled from here; later, the British used it for incarcerating — and hanging — political prisoners. Now the Prime Minister addresses the nation from its ramparts. **Opposite page:** *An aerial view of Chandni Chowk and Shahjahanabad. This crowded, dense urban sprawl was once the seventh city's chief artery, lyrically named the Path of the Moonbeams. Here the rich merchants had their mansions and ran a thriving trade; here flowed the Stream of Paradise from within the Red Fort in a manner designed by Shah Jahan's talented daughter, Princess Jahanara, who died in the service of her father; and it was this view that Mughal emperors commanded as they sat above the entrance to their fort to witness royal processions.*

reprisals were heavy. The famous poet of that time, Mirza Ghalib wrote, "Here there is a vast ocean of blood before me, God only knows what more I have still to behold." The British even wanted to convert the Jama Masjid into a church.

Most poignant was the fate of the last scion of the House of Timur, the shadow-king Bahadur Shah Zafar, who had dreamt of recapturing the days of Mughal glory, but had lost everything—the Peacock Throne, the historic Lal Qila and finally his kingdom. His two sons were brutally executed and he was humiliated and exiled to die at Rangoon, in Burma. He wrote from the depths of his sorrow:

Our Delhi was a garden city with peace pervading everywhere,
Its very name has been erased, naught save a crumbling ruin remains.

Since the turbulent time of Aurangzeb, the population of Delhi had been shrinking, though the city had continued to be an important political, cultural and literary centre. Now it came under British rule. The British had their headquarters at Calcutta, but preferred Delhi for their display of pomp and magnificence. In January 1877, Queen Victoria's assumption of the title of *Kaisar-i-Hind* (Empress of India) was marked by a week-long *durbar,* festivities and a spectacular procession through the Walled City. In 1903, Edward VII was proclaimed Emperor at an even grander *durbar.*

Then, in December 1911, when plague and famine were widespread, the third and most spectacular of the Delhi *durbars* was held; this time in the presence of King George V and his queen. The momentous announcement to move the British capital to Delhi was made at that *durbar.* The situation in Bengal was troubled; Delhi, which had a special place in Hindu and Muslim traditions, seemed the natural alternative. A town planning committee was set up to build New Delhi, even now one of the better planned cities of India.

The site chosen was the imposing Raisina hill, about 4 km south of Shahjahanabad. This was a well-drained and healthy area with ample room for future expansion. Over half a century ago the area was occupied by villages. The villages were cleared and the inhabitants shifted to a new site near the Yamuna. The architect, Sir Edwin Lutyens' remarkable conception of a garden city radiating from the Viceroy's residence (now Rashtrapati Bhawan, where the President of India lives) was formally inaugurated in 1930. All its roads had been designed at angles of sixty degrees).

In the early twentieth century, Delhi was caught up in the struggle for Indian independence. Being the capital, the city was the focus of political ferment. In 1912, a bomb was thrown at the Viceroy, Lord Hardinge, as he passed down Chandni Chowk on his elephant. Three revolutionaries were caught and sentenced to death by hanging. In 1922, Delhi was again the scene of bomb-throwing, this time in the Central Legislative Assembly. Bhagat Singh, one of the accused, is now a revered martyr.

Following the death of many Muslims in British firing inside the Walled City in 1919, Hindus and Muslims alike attended a funeral service at the Jama Masjid. But by 1922, communal disturbances had broken out in Delhi and some other towns. Gandhi undertook a twenty-one-day purification fast at Delhi.

When Gandhi launched his civil disobedience movement in 1930, liquor and foreign shops were picketed. Women laid themselves down in front of the shops selling foreign cloth around the clock tower in Chandi Chowk. A British resident recollects having walked over prostrate women to make a purchase. It is said that the women's jail at Lahore was soon filled by women

Delhi Museums

National Museum. The National Museum symbolizes the renewal of interest among Indians of India's classical heritage. The permanent collections of the museum encompass the vast canvas of India's heritage, from the age of the Indus Valley to modern times. Visiting exhibitions that are hosted by the museum from time to time expose visitors to the finest aesthetic traditions of India and the world.

The Indus Valley gallery has a collection of artefacts of that civilization and includes huge grain jars, seals, painted grey ware pottery, and statuary. A duplicate of the famous statue of a dancing girl is on display, the original being in safe keeping.

The museum also has a large collection of coins, statues, paintings of both Hindu and Buddhist inspiration from the Kushana, Gupta, Satavahana periods, to mention but a few. The Mughal period is represented in its famous miniatures, and jewellery, coins, tableware and other artefacts.

National Gallery Of Modern Art. The National Gallery of Modern Art is housed in Jaipur House near India Gate. The collection at the gallery is made up of paintings, sculptures and graphics representing the evolution of changing art forms over the last century. The collection is set out in a way that emphasizes the historical development of modern Indian art, and the display focuses on some of the most important schools of paintings such as the Bengal School and the Company School.

The gallery features collections of individual artists, both living and dead, such as Abanindranath Tagore, Rabindranath Tagore, Nandalal Bose, Jamini Roy, Amrita Shergil and M.F. Husain. The collection also includes sculptures and graphics by modern artists from all over the world. These are displayed in galleries adjoining the lawns of Jaipur House which have been developed into sculpture gardens.

National Handicrafts & Handlooms Museum. Situated in Pragati Maidan (Delhi's permanent trade fair complex), it was put together to serve as reference material for craftsmen who were increasingly losing touch with their own traditions in terms of materials and techniques because of the pressures of rapid industrialization. Every month this unique museum complex invites about fifty traditional artists and craftspersons from all over India to reside at the museum.

The museum's collection, built over a period of thirty years, has galleries given over to folk and tribal arts and crafts, and ritual artefacts, and others devoted to art forms in the great tradition. Traditional Indian textiles also have their separate galleries.

There are rare and distinctive pieces like the carved wooden figures of the *bhutas*, folk deities of coastal Karnataka, tribal bronzes from Madhya Pradesh and Orissa, and narrative paintings of pictorial story tellers.

A walk through the museum is a journey made through the streets of Jaisalmer, the temple courtyards of Madurai, the villages of Bani. There are old carved wooden doors and windows from Gujarat and Rajasthan, embroidered, beaded and painted wall hangings, embroideries, Kashmir shawls and applique work.

Nehru Memorial Museum & Library. Housed at Teen Murti, once the residence of India's first prime minister, it attracts a large number of tourists, children and other pleasure seekers, as well as research scholars. The former go there to see the collection of Nehru memorabilia which the museum hosts, or the Planetarium which is located on the premises, or the spectacular son et lumiere show. The latter visit the library which houses a vast collection of books, periodicals, archival newspapers and magazines, and documents of historical interest and importance.

Air Force Museum. Unveiled only recently, and located near the domestic terminal of the Indira Gandhi International Airport, it has put together a fascinating collection of models and memorabilia that reconstruct the history of the Indian Air Force.

The first section has models of every plane used by the Air Force until now. It also has the colours presented to the Indian Air Force by India's first President, Rajendra Prasad, in 1954, and pictures of war heroes who have done the force proud. The second section has a collection of photographs that depict the transition that the Indian Air Force underwent in the '50s, to cope with the needs of a newly-independent country. The last section familiarizes visitors with India's most recent and spectacular achievements in aviation and space travel. It includes photographs of the Soyuz T-11 spaceship, which was jointly launched by India and the Soviet Union, and, in which, for the only time in history, an Indian, Squadron Leader Rakesh Sharma, went into space.

The hangar outside the gallery also has a fascinating collection of vintage aircraft on display. The aircraft on display range between those used in the '20s to those used currently, and also includes a lifelike replica of the spaceship in which Neil Armstrong and others went to the moon.

For those who can find the time, visits are also recommended to such interesting museums as the ***Railway Museum*** with its rich collection of engines and coaches, including some of the oldest working models in the world; the ***Doll's Museum*** where dolls from all over the world fascinate a younger generation; ***Gandhi Smarak Sanghralaya*** close to Raj Ghat for Gandhi literature and memorabilia; and ***Safdarjung Museum*** where Indira Gandhi lived and was assasinated in 1984.

arrested in Delhi.

In 1945, in the precincts of the historic Lal Qila, the famous INA trial that rocked the country took place. The INA, the Indian National Army, had been founded abroad by Subhash Chandra Bose, with the slogan *Dilli Chalo*; "On to Delhi". The accused, who were followers of Bose, were defended by counsel Jawaharlal Nehru and a galaxy of Indian lawyer-statesmen. The tide had begun to turn against the British.

India became free on the stroke of midnight of 14-15 August 1947. At the Parliament House, the first Prime Minister, Jawaharlal Nehru, spoke movingly of the country's "tryst with destiny". The people of Delhi celebrated with tumultuous joy. But the exhilaration of independence was tempered by the pain of partition, caused by the formation of Pakistan. Gandhi was in Bengal; his presence maintaining peace between the communities. In Delhi riots broke out and only with Gandhi's coming to the city in September was peace restored.

Tragically, Gandhi paid with his life. On 30 January 1948, he was assassinated while at a prayer meeting. Delhi was plunged in grief. Pyarelal, his biographer, recounts the scene of Gandhi's funeral as the cortege passed near India Gate: "People had got on to the base of King George V's statue by wading through the surrounding pool. They hung on to the pillars surrounding the stone canopy, were seen perched on the top of the 150 feet high War Memorial, on the lamp or telephone posts and on the branches of the trees on both sides of the route to have a better view of the cortege. The entire central vista was a vast ant-heap of humanity, looking down from a distance, almost motionless." The Father of the Nation was cremated at Rajghat on the banks of the river Yamuna.

On 26 January 1950, India became a republic and adopted its Constitution. In those early years of independence, thousands of refugees from Pakistan poured into the city. The face of Delhi changed as new colonies sprawled out in all directions to accommodate the influx. Delhi was soon to become the first city of the country in all spheres of life.

ARCHITECTURE

"EVEN THE STONES HERE WHISPER TO our ears of the ages of long ago and the air we breathe is full of the dust and fragrance of the past," said Nehru. With its long and chequered history, Delhi is a city of monuments. The Archaeological Survey of India lists 1,300 monuments; some are magnificent works of architecture, others lie in ruins, and yet more are still in use hundreds of years after they were first built.

Centuries ago, when the Muslim invaders came to northern India, the foundations and pillars of every fort and stronghold taken were ground to powder under the heels of huge elephants. This is probably the reason why considerable areas in upper India are almost devoid of any Hindu architecture, especially around such early Islamic centres as Delhi and Ajmer. Later, temples and other structures were not ruthlessly demolished, but systematically taken apart and the pieces used in the new Islamic buildings. And still later, when Muslim presence in India had been consolidated, there was time for the rulers to plan and execute their buildings.

By the twelfth century, the indigenous art of building had already reached a high degree of perfection. Indian masons had had centuries of experience in creating monumental stone temples. When the Muslims came they brought with them the heritage of the great mosques of Samarqand, Cairo, Baghdad and Damascus, new principles and fresh ideas. The beam was replaced by the arch, the low-pointed temple roofs and spires gave way to domes and minarets. The skyline changed as the interactions between the Hindu and Muslim traditions reached an extraordinary synthesis in the time of the great Mughals.

The relics of Delhi's seven medieval cities — Lal Kot or Rai Pithora, Siri, Tughlakabad, Jahanpanah, Ferozabad, Purana Qila and Shahjahanabad—reflect every phase of Indo-Islamic architecture.

Approaching Delhi by air, one can see that the most striking landmark is the Qutb Minar, over 73 metres high and one of the most famous Muslim monuments in India. Most visitors begin a tour of Delhi's monuments here. Nearby is the ancient Rajput citadel of Qila Rai Pithora which has the

Facing page: *An exquisite representation in stone of Krishna lifting Mount Govardhan, a popular episode from the legends of the nation's favourite god.*
Preceding pages 18-19: *The devout congregate within Jama Masjid to offer their prayers during Id celebrations in the capital. As many as twenty thousand can gather in its courtyard around the obligatory water tank, facing west towards the cloister to kneel towards Mecca; the central arch is flanked on either side by five smaller arches ending in slender minarets that provide a feeling of grace to the three bulbous domes that crown the mosque. The 17th century Friday Mosque is now surrounded by crowded bazaars and is at the centre of social life in the Walled City.*

earliest extant Muslim monument in India, the Quwwat-ul-Islam mosque, built in 1139. It stands on the site of an old Jain temple. Built by Hindu craftsmen, the mosque has sculptured stone pillars from dismantled temples. It combines both local and Muslim building traditions. The arched stone screen façade, a later addition, has typically Hindu decorative floral motifs and typically Islamic low relief inscriptions. The famous iron pillar in the courtyard dates to the fourth century and is still uncorroded. It was evidently brought to Delhi by the city's founder, the Rajput chief, Anangpal. There is a belief that if you can encircle the pillar with your arms stretched out behind you, good luck is in store for you.

The Qutb Minar, perhaps initially a victory tower or an adjunct to the mosque for the priest to call the faithful to prayer, is made of red sandstone and tapers upwards. Begun by Qutb-ud-din in 1199 and completed by Iltutmish, the Qutb Minar is now five storeys high, though only the first storey is open to visitors.

Mehrauli, near the Qutb Minar, has several old monuments—a tomb which dates to Akbar's reign, many stepped wells built in the early years of Mughal rule, a large tank, the Hauz-i-Shamsi, built by Iltutmish in 1230. The site for this tank is said to have been suggested to the Sultan by the Prophet Muhammad himself who appeared to him in a dream. Its waters are believed to be sacred. On the banks of this tank is the Jahaz Mahal, built of grey and red sandstone. It perhaps derived its name from its ship-like appearance. Dated to the Lodi period (1451-1526), this monument is now used for the 'Phoolwalon ki Sair' festival.

A few kilometres north of the Qutb is Hauz Khas, the large tank which Ala-uddin Khalji built for the inhabitants of Siri. Feroz Shah Tughlak de-silted the tank and repaired it. The area to which this tank gives its name was till recently one of the numerous rural enclaves that still exist in the heart of the city. In 1988 a number of fashion designers, opened boutiques there. The success of these upmarket boutiques selling chic designer wear engendered a wave of similar shops. The government, taking cognizance of Hauz Khas's new-found

One of the many halls that are a feature of Rashtrapati Bhawan, once the residence of British Viceroys, now home to Indian Presidents. Displaying elements of Western classicism with Rajput and Mughal opulence, the palatial building has 340 rooms, is larger than the Versailles Palace and stretches 600 feet. To match its formal style, even the furniture was specially designed by Lutyens, and much of it has been retained.

***Facing page:** India Gate, the memorial arch built in the memory of the soldiers who died in the Second Afghan War, rises 139 feet high and is inscribed with the names of 13,000 Indian and British soldiers. It has a flame that burns eternally beneath the arch to commemorate the heroic sacrifices of the Indian army during its 1971 campaign against Pakistan.*

Less than a decade old, this gigantic statue of a Jain tirthankara placed atop the rocky ridge that rides from the Qutb Minar complex to the south-south cities of the modern capital, overlooks the 16th century tombs of Jamali-Kamali, the former a Sufi poet of repute. Nature lovers come here for bird-watching.

popularity have cleaned out the tank, illuminated the monuments, planted gardens and taken steps to maintain the complex. A dais has been erected there, and dance recitals are held on cool evenings against the backdrop of the illuminated monuments.

The most prominent of the buildings surrounding the tank is Feroz Shah's tomb; its lintel-spanned doorway and stone railings are characteristic of pre-Muslim Indian

The Lotus temple of the B'ahai faith, is set in a pool of water and surrounded by extensive gardens.

architecture which were adopted in Muslim buildings. To the north and west of the tomb is Feroz Shah's L-shaped *madrasa*, a school for religious instruction. Its hall and chambers, its lattice windows and deep niches for keeping books are quite unique. In 1398, when Timur invaded Delhi, he had camped at Hauz Khas.

It was the first of the Tughlaks, Ghiyas-ud-din, who built the fortress of Tughlakabad on a rocky hill, 8 km from the Qutb. This octagonal citadel with a perimeter of 6.5 km and rubble walls 10 to 15 metres high is almost completely in ruins. But strangely enough, Ghiyas-ud-din's tomb which was built in his lifetime is still intact. No satisfactory explanation is available for its unusually sloping walls. Another remarkable feature is the reappearance of the beam which is combined perfectly with the arch. Within the courtyard are solid underground vaults used, apparently, for hoarding the monarch's wealth. Ibn Batutah, a contemporary traveller, has written: "There he laid up great treasure....constructed a cistern and had molten gold poured into it so that it became one solid mass."

Three kilometres south-east of Tughlakabad, in the district of Gurgaon in Haryana, is Surajkund, a reservoir said to have been built by the legendary Surajpal of the Tomara dynasty in the tenth century. It is one of the few extant pieces of Hindu architecture in Delhi's neighbourhood. Its semi-circular stone embankment impounded the rain water from the Aravalli hills. A temple of the sun (Suraj) was said to exist to the west. Feroz Shah Tughlak, the great restorer of Delhi's buildings, repaired this tank too. Two kilometres south-west of Surajkund is the Anangpur dam across a narrow ravine, which irrigated the fields below. It is said to have been built by Anangpal, the founder of Delhi.

Moving northwards from Surajkund, towards the centre of Delhi, the visitor is drawn towards a dome of white marble. This is Humayun's tomb on the intersection of the Mathura and Lodi roads. Built in 1565 by the emperor's devoted wife Hamida, it is a landmark of Mughal architecture and a precursor of the Taj. It is Persian-inspired, yet it has much that is indigenous in its structure. A rudimentary concept of the garden tomb had existed in the Lodi period, but Humayun's mausoleum is the first tomb to have been built at the centre of a planned, square garden with a gateway in the middle of each of the four sides of the enclosure. The last of such tombs is that of Safdarjung (1735-54) which, however, is aesthetically far less pleasing.

Humayun's tomb stands on an elevated sandstone platform. The arcaded dais has several visitors' rooms. The arches of the platform are echoed on a larger scale in the tomb which too consists of a number of rooms, instead of being a single cell. The large dome consisting of a double shell appears for the first time outside of Persia, but the fanciful cupolas, or *chattris* are clearly Indian in origin. The combination of white marble and red sandstone facing, which was to have a tremendous influence on later Mughal architecture, is a testimony to the high skill of Indian craftsmen.

This tomb contains the remains of a galaxy of Mughal princes as well, many of whom met violent ends. It was also the scene of a poignant episode—the capture of the last Mughal emperor, Bahadur Shah, his two sons and grandson, who had taken refuge there during the 1857 uprising. The two sons and the grandson were sent to the gallows by Lt. Hodson and their bodies exposed to the people for twenty-four hours outside the Chandni Chowk police station.

Adjacent to Humayun's tomb is the *dargah* (shrine) of the Sufi saint Sheikh Nizam-ud-din Aulia, from whom the name of the modern residential colony nearby is derived. Nizam-ud-din died in 1325. The original tomb no longer exists; the present structure was built by a high-ranking devotee in 1526-63 and modified several times later. Twice a year, to mark the death anniversaries of Nizam-ud-din and the poet Amir Khusrau (who is buried close to Nizam-ud-din Auliya), a fair or *urs* is held here and attracts pilgrims from all over India.

There is a sacred *baoli* (stepped well) at the northern gate of the enclosure of the *dargah.* Legend has it that when the *baoli* was being built, Ghiyas-ud-din Tughlak was constructing Tughlakabad and forbade the labourers to work elsewhere. But the labourers worked for the saint by night. So the Sultan forbade the sale of oil. The labourers then used the well water instead of oil and it burned just as well.

Among the famous graves in the vicinity is a plain one of Jahanara, daughter of Shah Jahan: "Let naught cover my grave save the green grass; for grass well suffices a covering for the lowly," reads the inscription. There are also the tombs of two celebrated poets of Delhi, Amir Khusrau and Mirza Ghalib.

About 2 km west of the *dargah* of Nizam-ud-din Aulia are the Lodi Gardens and tombs. Formerly known as the Lady Willingdon Park, the Lodi Gardens contain several monuments. The most important of these is the tomb of Muhammad Shah, the Sayyid ruler who was the Sultan of Delhi from 1434 to 1444. The Bara Gumbad and Masjid date to the time of Sikandar Lodi (1489-1517). This tomb is of an unidentified high official and the mosque built in 1494 was perhaps an adjunct to the tomb. Similar to the Bara Gumbad is the Sheesh Gumbad or Glass Dome which has several graves. However, none of the graves have been identified. The Sheesh Gumbad too is ascribed to Sikandar Lodi's reign. Its dome has artistic floral motifs and inscriptions from the Koran engraved on it. When the monument was constructed, the architect had the dome covered with blue tiles. These

The observatory or Jantar Mantar, constructed by Sawai Jai Singh of Jaipur, in the heart of New Delhi. The ruler was able to unravel many astronomical mysteries with the help of his giant mason instruments.

Soon after independence, Mahatma Gandhi was assassinated while on his way to a prayer meeting. His simple memorial by the banks of the Yamuna is a simple flower-strewn platform, inscribed with the phrase he most often used at prayer meetings — 'He Ram'.

Preceding pages 26-27: *This canopy once housed a statue of King George, removed upon independence. Today, it is argued that such a canopy would do injustice to an Indian leader's statue for the opulence of its setting; yet to remove the canopy itself would desecrate the newly built city on which 15 million had been spent till the time of its inauguration in 1936. Had the National Stadium not been built at the head of the road, the view would have encompassed Purana Qila as anticipated by Lutyens.*

reflected the sunlight, giving the appearance of a glass dome. Sikandar Lodi's own tomb, an octagonal structure, is set amidst a square garden within high walls—an early rudimentary garden tomb. In the present Lodi Gardens can also be found an ancient bridge, the Athpula, a bridge of eight piers, one of the many bridges built in Mughal times. The Athpula is dated to Akbar's time in the latter half of the sixteenth century.

Further west is the double-storeyed tomb of the Nawab of Safdarjung, the prime minister of the Mughal emperor, Muhammad Shah. It is the last instance of a garden tomb. It was built soon after Safdarjung's death in 1753-54, and lacks the harmonious proportions of Humayun's tomb built nearly two centuries earlier.

Proceeding northwards along Mathura Road, a part of the Grand Trunk Road (now known as the Sher Shah Road), you come to the ruins of the Purana Qila, the Old Fort, on a small hill overlooking the Zoological Park. This was the city that Sher Shah (1538-45) built by demolishing Humayun's Dinpanah, on the site of the Pandava's capital, Indraprastha. The western gate of the 2 km long ramparts is of sandstone and topped by cupolas. It is possible that Humayun either repaired or completed the Purana Qila when he recaptured the city. Among the few buildings that have survived within the fort is the Sher-e-Mandal, the two-storeyed octagonal tower which Humayun used as a library. The Qila-e-Kuhna Masjid, with its arched bays, marks an important phase in the development of the mosque and the transition from pre-Mughal styles.

The excavated site of the Purana Qila is perhaps even more interesting. Some trial trenches were dug on the south-eastern side in 1955. Painted Grey Ware dated 1000 BC was revealed, besides relics of later periods. Excavations between 1969 and 1973 showed a continuous stratification from Mauryan to early Mughal times.

Among the objects found were hard, glossy earthenware pottery of the Mauryas (circa 3000 BC). There was copper currency of the Saka-Kushan age (100 BC-AD 300), a gold-plated Gupta coin (*circa* AD 400-600) and damaged stone sculptures of the post-Gupta period (*circa* AD 700-800).

Above and facing page: *The view from Jama Masjid encompasses the city, showing, to one side, the old city and the domes of the mosque; on the other, the emerging modern city with its secular architecture.*

Other finds included a Rajput-built rubble wall (AD 900-1200) and glazed ware used in the Delhi Sultanate (AD 1206-1526). Artefacts of the early Mughal period were revealed in a refuse dump of discarded household items. These included painted Chinese Ming porcelain, wine bottles and a gold earring inlaid with pearls and emeralds. Indeed, if you had to look for the story of Delhi in any one place, that would be the Purana Qila.

Continuing northwards from the Purana Qila, you come to Feroz Shah Kotla. According to contemporary historians, Ferozabad, the city that Feroz Shah Tughlak built, extended from Hauz Khas to the northern ridge. All that now remains is his citadel, then on the banks of the river Yamuna. In medieval times all the Mathura road monuments were flanked on their eastern side by the river. But the Yamuna now flows a more easterly course, considerably away from the buildings.

Feroz Shah was a passionate builder, but his eccentric predecessor, Muhammad bin Tughlak, had emptied the coffers and so Feroz Shah had to use rough rubble instead of fine sandstone, and eschew the highly decorative Indian masonry. However, his citadel is an early instance of the Islamic palace-fort which was to develop so splendidly in the time of Akbar and Shah Jahan. Atop a three-storey pyramidal structure in the citadel is a 45 metre high Ashokan pillar weighing 23 tons which the Sultan had removed from Ambala in the Punjab, transported 200 km by river and re-erected in Delhi. The deciphering of the Ashokan edicts on this column in the nineteenth century provided the key to the Brahmi script.

The striking gate, once known as Kabuli Darwaza, that stands just outside Maulana Azad Medical College and very near Feroz Shah Kotla on Bahadur Shah Zafar Marg, was probably one of the gates to the citadel of Purana Qila built by Sher Shah. The 'Bloody Gate' or Khuni Darwaza, as it is popularly known, has witnessed a lot of bloodshed. After Aurangzeb defeated his brother Dara Shikoh in a war of succession, the latter was beheaded and his head was displayed at this gate—a warning to all pretenders to the throne. The last heirs to the

Mughal empire too were hung to death here.

To the north of Feroz Shah Kotla is one of the finest achievements of Indo-Islamic architecture in the city, the Lal Qila or Red Fort of Shah Jahan, the great Mughal builder. He transferred his capital from Agra to Delhi in 1638 and laid the foundations of Shahjahanabad. A year later he began the Red Fort, an imposing palace-fort measuring 900 metres by 550 metres. It took nine years to complete. The Red Fort is aligned from north to south with the river on the east and the Lahori Gate entrance on the west. Beyond the gate and within the fort is the Chatta Chowk, a vaulted arcade which used to be a bazaar in Mughal times, with shops for the court jewellers, goldsmiths, enamel workers, miniature artists, carpet weavers and brocade weavers.

Within the walls of Red Fort, at one of the entrance gates into the apartments : the 17th century fort completed in 1648 was twice the size of that in Agra, though like the latter it was sited on the banks of the Yamuna. Richly embellished by apartments, sadly many of these were destroyed under British occupation who also left behind ugly barrack buildings as remnants of their own occupation of the fort.

The Diwan-i-Am (Hall of Public Audience) is at the centre of the fort. It was originally ornamented with gold and precious stones and hung with brocaded velvet from Turkey and silk from China. In the alcove above the throne is a small Florentine panel of the Greek God Orpheus and his lute. This was probably acquired in trade and used "just as a piece of exotic brocade might be included in a patchwork quilt." The Diwan-i-Am, a hall with rows of columns, is raised on a plinth with three sides open. Ceremonial events were conducted in the hall.

On the eastern side of the fort are the marble palaces, facing the ornamental courtyards. The most striking are the Diwan-i-Khas (Hall of Private Audience) and the Rang Mahal (Painted Palace). The Diwan-i-Khas, with its costly silver ceiling, studded with tiny pieces of mirror, reflects thousands of lights when a candle is lighted. Its inlaid floral designs, its gilded arches and polished marble have witnessed the rise and fall of the Mughals. The spirit of this architectural wonder is captured in the inscriptions engraved above the arches:

Agar firdaus bar ru-yi-zamin ast,
Hamin ast, u hamin ast, u hamin ast.
(If on Earth be an Eden of bliss,
It is this, it is this, none but this.)

Important matters of state were discussed by the emperor inside this pavilion. The famous Peacock Throne, worth about twelve million pounds sterling, stood within the hall. It was Nadir Shah who, after plundering the city, carried away the throne to Persia in 1739. In 1857, it was at the Diwan-i-Khas that Emperor Bahadur Shah was tried and exiled. The story of the Red Fort, with its palaces and *hammams* (baths), its fountains and flowing streams, and its later addition, the Pearl Mosque or Moti Masjid, is recaptured today in a sound and light spectacle, the *son et lumiere*. The two museums at the Red Fort have some exquisite Mughal miniature paintings, rare manuscripts, dresses, coins and armoury.

Shah Jahan also gave Delhi the historic city of Shahjahanabad with its main street, Chandni Chowk, leading from the Lahori Gate of the Red Fort to the Fatehpuri Masjid (mosque) in the west. At its eastern end is a Jain temple and a unique bird hospital. Further down is the historic Gurudwara

Sisganj where the ninth Sikh Guru, Tegh Bahadur, was beheaded in 1657 by Aurangzeb. In some ways this bustling commercial centre, known for its silver and gold embroidery and its ivory carving, has not changed since Mughal days when the French traveller Bernier described the "open shops where during the day, artisans work, bankers sit for the dispatch of business and merchants exhibit their wares."

Within Shahjahanabad or the Walled City, about 900 metres west of the Red Fort, is the Jama Masjid (Friday Mosque), the largest in India. It was begun by Shah Jahan in 1650 and is said to have taken 5,000 workers six years to complete. It stands on a plinth, its high platform reached by a flight of steps. Its 1,000 sq m courtyard is enclosed by pillared corridors with domed pavilions at the corners. There is an old map of the world engraved on one of the pillars. Its prayer hall has a spectacular arched façade and a pulpit carved out of a single marble block. The mosque is still one of the main congregational centres for Muslims in the city. In one of the corner rooms are preserved footprints of Prophet Hazrat Muhammad.

The Walled City suffered terribly during the 1857 uprising and its aftermath. Towards the north-west of Shahjahanabad on the northern ridge is a red stone tower, now known as Ajitgarh. A plaque was fixed here in 1972 in memory of those who rose against colonial rule. Originally, the tapering tower was the Mutiny Memorial built in 1863 by the British in memory of the officers and men killed in the siege of Delhi.

On the crest of the ridge near the University of Delhi is another circular tower commemorating the site where British women and children had gathered during the uprising before they fled to Karnal in Haryana. This was also the point where the rebel Indian soldiers made their last stand before they fell behind the city walls.

Due south from the northern ridge is the majestic red and cream sandstone Rashtrapati Bhawan. Designed as the home of the British Viceroys, it is now the official residence of the President of India. It is one of the largest buildings of its kind and took eight years (1921-29) and 14 million rupees to complete. Its first occupant was Lord Irwin.

Sir Edwin Lutyens, the British architect, combined in this building the best of both Indian and Western architecture—the symmetry borrowed from Mughal architecture, the dome from Buddhist stupas, the 227 columns from the Greeks and Romans, the 35 loggias from the Italians and the beautiful courts from the English.

Having overcome the problem of choosing an appropriate design reflecting "the eternal beauty of classical architecture with appropriate features of Indian architecture grafted on it," Sir Edwin Lutyens and Sir Herbert Baker went around hunting for possible sites. The authorities approved of a site which was several kilometres away from the present location of the Rashtrapati Bhawan. Lutyens felt dejected for he had set his heart on Raisina hill. After consultations with Baker, Lutyens decided to go ahead with his own plans. One fine night,

The high, vaulted-ceiling of the Anglican Church combines natural and artificial light to provide a cheerful, if formal, seating in pews for Delhi's Christian community.

Popular cinema would probably top the list as favourite entertainment for most people in Delhi. Not only are film stars adulated, cinema halls boast hoardings that are an example of a pop-art transforming actors into demi-gods. When an expected blockbuster is released, tickets for the shows are difficult to come by and can at best be obtained in 'black', a system whereby touts buy up all available seats and then auction them to buyers at the highest bidding.

Lutyens and Baker moved the two foundation stones over to Raisina hill. Forests were cleared and temporary rail lines were laid to bring in the sandstone from Bharatpur and Dholpur. Kilns were fired to manufacture the 700 million bricks required for the New Delhi city centre. In January 1931, the city of New Delhi was inaugurated. This was the eighth city of Delhi.

Rashtrapati Bhawan faces east and its central axis, Rajpath, leads straight to India Gate or the War Memorial arch. The Central Secretariat buildings are on the north and south of Rajpath. Each year on 26 January, when India's Republic Day is celebrated, Rajpath is bedecked for the occasion. All along the road the Indian tricolour flutters from the lamp-posts as the President arrives in state. The caparisoned elephants, the stately cavalry, the orderly military units, the singing school children, the colourful bands, the gaily decorated floats and finally the magnificent fly-past by fighter aircraft—all these together create the kind of spectacle which the British architects had envisaged.

In the same complex is the circular Parliament House with Parliament Street leading in the direction of the Jama Masjid. To the western side of Rashtrapati Bhawan are the terraced Mughal Gardens. The whole complex of buildings is occidental, with some traditional Indian elements included.

India Gate was designed by Sir Edwin Lutyens and its foundation was laid in 1921 by, the Duke of Connaught. It was completed ten years later. Rising to a height of 42 metres, it is a memorial to the 90,000 Indian soldiers who died in the Second Afghan War. The names of British and Indian officers killed on the North-West Frontier are engraved on the memorial. Under the arch, a lamp burns perpetually beside an inverted rifle and helmet, and men of the Indian Army, Navy and Air Force stand in ceremonial guard at the site.

In conception and character, New Delhi follows an essentially classical plan. Though the city has since expanded, and new office buildings have come up, the colonial grandeur remains in its wide tree-lined avenues, stately white colonnaded buildings and residences, spacious gardens and driveways. At the far end of Parliament Street is New

Delhi's chief shopping centre, the horse-shoe shaped Connaught Place, with its wide colonnaded verandahs typical of the period.

In striking contrast, about 250 metres south of Connaught Place, is the Jantar Mantar observatory built by Maharaja Jai Singh II of Jaipur in 1719. The massive masonry instruments consist of the Samrat Yantra, an equinoctial dial, the Jai Prakash, made of two concave hemispheres to tell the position of the sun and other heavenly bodies, and several other instruments. Similar observatories were later built by Jai Singh at Jaipur, Ujjain, Varanasi and Mathura.

The Lotus Temple in Kalkaji, located in the extreme south of the city, is one of the newest architectural attractions of Delhi. This temple built by the Baha'i community, an eclectic and catholic sect originating in Iran with an international following, is built in the shape of a budding lotus set amidst a pool of water, and is built entirely of marble. Designed with the help of computers, it is surrounded by well-manicured lawns, is manned by volunteers who lead visitors into the hall where one can meditate in peace, and is open to adherents of all faiths. It houses no idols in keeping with the tenets of the faith.

At the international centre for the study of Buddhism, on the Mehrauli road near Qutb Minar, the Buddha shrine has images from all parts of the world. There is the Indian Buddha in a typically meditative posture, a Cambodian Buddha standing with a begging bowl in hand and images from Thailand and Burma. Besides these, there is a small Buddha temple adjacent to the Lakshmi Narayan temple on Mandir Marg. On the banks of the Yamuna is the Ladakh Buddha Vihara built in the characteristic Ladakhi style with prayer flags fluttering in the wind. This monastery has a large Buddha image and its saffron-clad monks study and meditate on the teachings of the Buddha.

The site on the banks of the Yamuna where Mahatma Gandhi was cremated on the evening of 31 January 1948, has been consecrated as a *samadhi.* It consists of a raised platform of black marble. On this is inscribed the last words which he had uttered on being assassinated: *He Ram* (Hail God). Every year on his death anniversary

The new business in the capital is tourism, and one of its major fallouts is shopping. The painted walls of this Delhi crafts emporium wittily recreate the city's long tradition of courtiers and kings.

SUPER

Right: *Birju Maharaj, a Kathak dancer, at a performance in Delhi. Delhi is now the cultural capital of the country where every performer must make his mark before winning national or international accolades.*
Preceding pages 34-35: *An overview of Connaught Place, the three-concentric ringed commercial heart of the city named after the Duke of Connaught by the British who had it laid in sharp contrast to the typical Indian bazaars of Chandni Chowk.*

(30th January), and his birth anniversary (2 October), special functions are held there and thousands come to pay homage.

HERITAGE

IN THE SHADOW OF THE JAMA MASJID, grizzled old Khyamuddin works in a tiny room reached by a nearly perpendicular flight of steps. Through the window you can glimpse the minarets of the mosque reaching out to the sky over the cramped rooftops. A bright red *dupatta* is stretched across a wooden embroidery frame. Khyamuddin sits crouched over a panel depicting a silver and green peacock against the background of an improbable forest, as his wife puts the finishing touches to velvet and *zari* (gold or silver thread) evening bags and belts. The phenomenal rise in gold and silver prices has made real *zari* a thing of the past; copper-plated *zari* and silken threads from Surat in Gujarat are used. This exquisite craft which has come down from Mughal times is also on the decline. Despite the uncertainties and low returns, Khyamuddin and the 5,000 other *zari* workers of Delhi are proud of their *khandani,* the heritage of their forefathers.

Delhi's heritage goes back several centuries, a heritage that is an amalgamation of two very rich traditions. The fourth and fifth centuries saw the flowering of Hindu culture under the Guptas. The Muslims brought with them their own exotic traditions. What emerged from the combination of both was one of the richest cultures in the world. This was at its peak during the rule of Emperor Shah Jahan. The glory of the Mughal courts is indeed legendary. Lavish court patronage and the life-style of the nobility nourished crafts that have long since vanished. In Delhi a few survive today. Khyamuddin's is one such.

In the golden days of Shahjahanabad, a variety of crafts flourished. The manufacture of *varak,* fine decorative beaten gold or silver spread on Indian sweets, was popular. It is said that Bahadur Shah Zafar, the last Mughal Emperor, gave a feast of more than 500 dishes for which he had over 100 kg of gold beaten into *varak.* Gold *varak* is no longer available but silver *varak* is still made on a small scale. The Walled City has also perfected the art of turban making, which comes down from pre-Muslim days. *Pugrees* (turbans), coloured masks and headgear for a variety of festivals are still made. Marble filigree and copper engraving were among Delhi's finest crafts. But through the years the city's craftsmen have moved away to other centres in northern India or taken to different occupations. Some marble workers can still be seen at work, as can the *meenakari* workers. *Meenakari* is enamel work on burnished gold.

The standard of leather craft is still maintained; though the *jooties* (slip-on shoes) of Jaipur and the shoes of Agra have become more famous, people still come to Delhi to buy slippers. "Nothing could be prettier or more dainty than some of the slippers made for native ladies' wear, embroidered with seed pearls, usually false, with spangles and every variety of gold and silver thread and inlaid with red, black or emerald green leather in decorative patterns," wrote an appreciative European.

Some of the magic of Delhi's ancient crafts and pastimes can still be glimpsed in the streets and bylanes of the Walled City, in Hauz Qazi and Ballimaran; in Kinari Bazaar and the Dariba jewellery market. But much too has been lost. The medieval sports of *kabutarbazi* (a contest of

pigeons), *patangbazi* (kite-flying contests), and cock and quail fights are now rare. The music of the dancing girls is fading but the *quwwalis* and the *ghazal* sessions retain their irresistible popularity.

In the cultural season in winter, several classical music festivals are held, where the cream of north Indian and Carnatic or south Indian musicians can be heard. Delhi has also witnessed a resurgence of the classical dance: the sculpturesque Bharata Natyam of the south, the graceful, flowing style of Odissi from Orissa, the north Indian Kathak with its enchantingly rhythmic footwork and the subdued eloquence of the Manipuri style from the north-east. Many renowned gurus have left their home states to teach music and dance in Delhi.

If Delhi's new cultural activities are restricted to its educated and well-to-do residents, not so its religion-inspired fairs and festivals which draw all sections of society. Every Indian religious denomination has a holy place in Delhi: the Muslims have the Jama Masjid, the Idgah and several other mosques; the Hindus have the Lakshmi Narayan temple, the Hanuman temple and the Kali Devi temple and a multitude of small shrines. The Catholics, Protestants and Syrian Christians have their own churches. There is a Buddhist shrine at the Ladakh Buddha Vihara; there is a Jain temple, and a Zoroastrian fire temple too in the city. The Sikhs, who constitute a major part of Delhi's population, have several *gurudwaras*, chiefly the Sisganj, the Rakabganj and the Bangla Sahib.

With this varied population, hailing from all the states of India, Delhi celebrates a number of festivals. The chief of these are the Muslim Id, the Hindu festival of lights, Diwali, and Dussehra, besides national anniversaries such as Republic Day on 26 January. Of all these it is perhaps Dussehra or Ram Leela which touches the very core of Delhi. The festival of the nine nights of the ten days marks the victory of good over evil. In the finale of the Ram Leela, gigantic effigies of Ravana and his fellow *rakshasas* (demons) go up in flames as Ram shoots at them with a symbolic arrow, marking the climax of the epic, the *Ramayana*. Lately Delhi has also seen the revival and strengthening of folk traditions.

It is not impossible to see the world without stepping out of the Indian capital. In a few years alone, Delhi has made its mark in international polity and culture, and in the winter season is the venue for a host of events from round the world. The best theatre, ballet, music and dance can be seen live on its stage just as museums and art galleries feature special retrospectives from around the globe.
Overleaf: *Nor does Delhi lack in entertainment choices. While residents often refer to the capital as a city that tucks in with the television at nine o' clock sharp, there is in truth enough for the visitor to discover when the stars are out. There is theatre, Indian dance and music, nightclub dining, and discotheques, such as Annabelles at the Holiday Inn Crowne Plaza.*

Walking Through Delhi's History

TRAVEL AGENCIES IN DELHI offer the visitor fairly standardised half-day tours of 'Old' and 'New' Delhi. These terms refer to municipal divisions by which north Delhi is 'Old' and south 'New'. In actual fact, in Delhi old and new are geographically intermeshed. The Delhi Development Authority has designated some areas as 'conservation zones' but these are not hived off from the rest of the city. The visitor who has a little time to spare will enjoy walking through different historic areas. He should be armed with a good street-map (the Survey of India has a good *Tourist Map*), a copy of the map of *Delhi Monuments* prepared by the Archaeological Survey, a flask of water and stout shoes. The suggested walks should not take more than two hours each; the visitor will see less than he would on a whistle-stop taxi tour, but he will remember more.

Mostly 13th century. Start at the *Qutb Minar,* walk through the Quwwat-ul-Islam Masjid of which it is the corner minaret, cross over to the unfinished Alai Minar and see the exquisitely-carved tomb of Iltutmish. Returning to the Minar, you can strike off to the south, past the dilapidated grey-white tomb which Charles Metcalfe used as his week-end cottage, to Jamali-Kamali, a lovely early Mughal mosque, adjacent to which is the tomb of the great poet Jamali, in a tiny structure which is covered with stucco decoration like a Persian carpet. From here you have a choice: you can strike off to the east to the motor-road, and walk to the Buddha Vihara, or go west toward the village of Mehrauli. The path winds through scrub and wood, and it is a pleasant surprise to reach a clearing where stands a beautiful stepwell many storeys deep, with a small tomb nearby. A few yards away is the Mehrauli bus-stand, dominated by the massive octagonal tomb of Adham Khan (Mughal, 16th century). If you walk down the bazaar street, ask to see the shrine of Bakhtiyar Kaki. If you have time, go further down the bazaar to Jahaz Mahal and Hauz Shamsi where the Phulwalon ki Sair is held every October.

14th century. Tughlakabad is a magnificent fort which deserves a leisurely walk. Largely in ruins, and hemmed in by fields and a village which cover the area of the town which surrounded the fort, it calls for an active imagination to see this as it was. It used to be entered through successive halls to the south and not (as at present) through the rear gate on the east. Its different levels lead up to the high point which the king used for ceremonial occasions. Ask the *chowkidar* to show you the cavernous water-reservoir and the opening of the tunnel leading out. Leaving the fort, walk across the causeway to Ghiyas-ud-din's tomb; at the time of building, a sheet of water separated the fort and the tomb. If you walk on the wide parapet of the defensive wall, you can see the openings of the chambers for storing grain. The small ruined fort to the east is Adilabad, also 14th century, making this an unusual complex of fortified structures.

More 14th century. If you would like to see more of the Tughlaks' sturdy rubble-built architecture, you could explore the remains of the city of Jahanpanah. Start with Vijay Mandal, south of Sarvapriya Vihar (opposite Panchsheel Club). It is not a fort, but there are similarities with Tughlakabad in its stepped construction, from the flat plain where stood the Hall of the Thousand Pillars, through successive chambers to the final small chamber at the summit from which the Sultan reviewed troops, and from where today we get a splendid view of south Delhi. The palace of the Tughlaks is today a cricket pitch for the children of Begumpur village nearby. Ask them to direct you to the nearby Begumpur Masjid, a multi-domed mosque with a majestic *aiwan,* a tall archway, in front of the sanctum sanctorum. Like all Delhi monuments this has access to the roof. A scooter-ride can then take you past Lal Gumbad (Red Dome, a tomb with the same sloping batter as Ghiyas-ud-din's tomb near Tughlakabad) to Khirki Masjid on the Saket road. Built under the patronage of the same minister who commissioned Begumpur Masjid, this is an unusual mosque with a cruciform layout, and windows (*khirki*). A few yards down the road is Satpula, the remains of a sluice gate which regulated the water-supply to the Tughlak city.

15th century. Lodi Garden offers a very comfortable walk. The name is misleading

because the garden was laid out by the British to mark the southern boundary of Lutyens' Delhi, by clearing the area of the village that inhabited it. Start at the northern end, from Athpula (eight piers to Satpula's seven) and then go up the steps to *Sikander Lodi's tomb*, set in a garden, a tranquil retreat. Wander through the garden, landscaped by Delhi-based American architect Joseph Stein (who has also designed the nearby India International Centre) to Sheesh and Bara Gumbads, sparing time for a look at the small cluster of Mughal buildings off to the left. Follow the path to the octagonal Syed tomb and Stein's glass-house. Leave the garden, turn right and walk to Safdarjang's Tomb, set in a spacious garden (18th century) and notice the office of the Archaeological Survey in the pavilions along the southern boundary walls.

16th century. Purana Qila is a small enclosed fort, but there is a lot you can explore. After you enter, you will instinctively make your way to the splendid Qila-e-Kuhna (corner) Masjid; after you have had your fill of it, don't miss the deep stepwell in the middle of the garden, and the *hammam* (bath) in front of the Sher Mandal, where Humayun's manuscript library used to be. Spend some time looking at the birds in the nearby zoo from the southern ramparts. You can walk along the eastern ramparts too, but be careful, because they are broken in many places. Remember to see the Museum before it closes at 5 pm (and also on Mondays). After you come out, have a look at the beautiful northern gate (which is never opened), and follow the wall clockwise. You can cross the road for a visit to the lovely Crafts Museum (again closes at 5 pm).

16th century. Humayun's Tomb is one of the most beautiful buildings in India, and you should take some time taking it in. It has an unusually long approach, with ornate gateways. Allow yourself to be diverted to the right at the first gateway, to Isa Khan's tomb and mosque. Through an opening in the wall you reach Arab Serai. These and other buildings to the east give you an idea of the morphology of the city then, with buildings and enclosures built

adjacent to each other, not separated by streets. After you have studied Humayun's tomb, exit from the *southern* gateway into the pleasant modern housing estate called Nizamuddin East, and make your to the tomb of Abdur Rahim Khan-e-Khanan, a great Mughal general best remembered for his limpid poetry in Hindi. If you have time, you can cross the busy Mathura Road to Nizamuddin West, and enter the totally different ambience of the area around the shrine of Nizamuddin, redolent with the smell of roses mingling with that of freshly-baked bread.

17th century. Shahjahanabad as a walker's delight is the subject of an excellent book by Gaynor Barton and Lorraine Malone *(Ten Easy Walks in Old Delhi)*. If you can spare time for only *one* walk, you could walk up (east to west) along Chandni Chowk, noticing its special feature, of having places of worship of five religions along its length. When you reach the Town Hall, a British building, you can take a loop to the right to see the railway station, another proud British contribution, and come back to Fatehpuri Masjid; take a sniff at the adjacent Khari Baoli market, where you will be assailed by the fragrance of a hundred spices. A walk through the narrow Nai Sarak (the textbook bazaar) and the Chawri Bazaar (paper market) with their innumerable culs-de-sac enclosing still more shops, brings you up to the grandeur of *Jama Masjid*. If it is not near the time for prayers, you can climb the minaret for a

wonderful view of the city. Karim's restaurant nearby will give you superb Mughlai cuisine. If it is getting to dusk, you can then go to Lal Qila for the *son-et-lumiere* show. To see the Lal Qila itself will be a separate walk.

19th century. 'Mutiny' buffs will enjoy a walk on the Ridge near Delhi University. This is beautifully landscaped, very different from the hot rocky nightmare of 1857. On University Road, walk to the Flagstaff Tower; then take the path to the west to the remains of the Chauburji mosque which also figures in Mutiny lore. Cross the road and make for Bara Hindu Rao, now a hospital but with the ruins of a Tughlak hunting-lodge nearby. This is worth climbing for a spectacular view of Delhi, though not of tigers. Nearby is an Ashoka pillar, and the Mutiny Memorial in Victorian neo-Gothic.

20th century. Lutyens' city is a pedestrian's delight, with its wide pavements shaded with leafy trees selected by Lutyens himself. The *minimum* is Rajpath. Start at the Canopy where the statue of George V used to stand. Baroda House and Hyderabad House, at the ends of two of the radial roads from India Gate, are Lutyens' work.

Walk down the lawns, past the Boat Club, the Hyde Park Corner of Delhi, lively with political demos and speeches when Parliament is in session, up past the baroque fountains again designed by Lutyens, to the open area of Vijay Chowk. If you can brave the traffic and walk along the central yellow line, you will enjoy seeing the trick of the gradient, when Rashtrapati Bhavan sinks and all but disappeares, only to reappear when you have crested the hill. Baker's Secretariats lie on either side of you, and the expanse of the President's House in front. Take the side entrance to the right, and walk through the grounds till you reach the side gate which leads to the elegant and peaceful Church of the Redemption, designed by Medd.

AGRA

The Romance of Marble

With narrow, serpentine streets, crowded, bustling bazaars; spacious suburbs and a fine cantonment; this teeming city on the banks of the river Yamuna, 200 km south of Delhi, is like any other Indian settlement — and yet it is not. For this is Agra, the city of one of the wonders of mankind — the shimmering white jewel, the Taj Mahal.

"The earliest mention of Agra is in the epic *Mahabharata* (third century BC). It was then called Agrabana, Sanskrit for Paradise. In the second century AD, Ptolemy, the geographer of Alexander the Great, showed it on his map of the world as Agra." But it was only at the turn of the fourteenth century that the city appears on the map of India. Three hundred and fifty years ago, at the height of Mughal power, Agra was the imperial capital and the largest and most important city of northern India. It was here that the famous school of Mughal painting was founded and flourished. And it was here, under Emperor Akbar, that a unique synthesis of Indian and Persian thought and culture was achieved in the latter half of the sixteenth century. This blend of two traditions found expression in all walks of life, from the architecture of Fatehpur Sikri and the lovely Mughal miniatures to the eclectic religion, Din-i-Ilahi, founded by Akbar.

The best way to get to Agra is from Delhi, with the Mughal monuments in the capital forming a prelude — or an hors d'oeuvre if you prefer — to the magnificence of the Taj. With the Mughals dividing their time between their forts at Delhi, Agra and Lahore (now in Pakistan), and their summers in Kashmir, it is exciting to imagine that the route we take today, and which forms part of the famed Grand Trunk Road of Sher Shah Suri, must have been witness to innumerable imperial processions. On elephant and horseback in palanquins and in carriages, the Mughals must have journeyed, complete with their harems; so too must their armies have marched, setting camp along the route, the hardships of the journey in no manner detracting from the luxuries of the royal entourage. For, the emperor and empress and other members of the inner court, the ministers and officials were accompanied by the finest cooks, their entertainers and dancing girls, slaves and concubines.

Modern Agra is, for most part, an eyesore, with characterless lanes and bazaars, and a cantonment that though leafy and spacious, creates no distinctive impressions. Yet, here is the flowering of the finest Mughal architecture that no other city — not Delhi, not Lahore — can boast of . For besides the Taj, there is the creative vision of Sikandra and Itmad-ud-Daulah, the grandeur of Agra Fort, as well as a wealth of smaller tombs and mosques. And finally, it may truly be said that years from now visitors will come not to see the Taj but Dayal Bagh, a monument that has been in the making since the turn of the century, and which when complete, will have used more marble than the Taj, and with greater atten-

Facing page: *The Taj Mahal must be the world's most perfect building, totally proportionate in its physical surroundings and combining elements of Indian architecture with the Mughal love of decoration. While the sensitive view it as an abiding symbol of an emperor's love for his wife, it is not difficult to understand a recent poet's admission that the Taj makes a mockery of the love of the poor.*
This page: *Detail from the marble screen that surrounds the cenotaphs within the Taj Mahal. The cenotaphs are enclosed within an octagonal fretted marble screen that alone took ten years in the making, and besides its lace-like carving, is consistent in its use of pietra-dura inlay setting precious and semi-precious stones in marble , each decorative element rated individually as a work of art.*

When the third Mughal began work on his first fort in Agra, the roots of the dynasty were strong enough to demand an imperial residence worthy of their holdings in Hindustan. Begun in 1565, Agra Fort ***(above)*** *became the centre of Mughal dominion over the subcontinent for well over a century. It was founded by Akbar who equipped the fort with as many as five hundred apartments. With rare exceptions such as Jehangiri Mahal* ***(top)****, little has survived for the emperor was followed by two of India's greatest builders, Jehangir and Shah Jahan, who between themselves totally changed the fort interiors.*

tion to detail.

Indeed, Agra, the city of beautiful buildings, has much to offer besides the Taj Mahal, even if it is for the Taj that it is best remembered.

HISTORY

THE CITY OF AGRA WAS FOUNDED IN the early years of the sixteenth century, at a time when the authority of the Delhi Sultanate, then under the control of the Lodis, was fast disappearing. The last Lodi Sultan was overthrown by an adventurer from Central Asia. This was Babar, the founder of the Mughal dynasty in the Indian subcontinent.

Babar did not like India. In his memoirs he complained that India had no good horses, no dogs, no grapes, musk-melons or good fruit, no ice or cold water, no bread or cooked food in the bazaars, no hot baths, no colleges, no candles. Above all, Babar missed the mountainous terrain of Farghana, now a province of Chinese Turkistan, where he had grown up. To increase the charm of his surroundings, Babar laid out a beautiful garden, the Rambagh at Agra. Symmetrical pathways, running water and fountains, beds of roses and narcissi: the Persian garden had come to India.

After Babar's death at Agra in 1530, Humayun was left with a precarious hold on the kingdom. A modern commentator writes: "In Agra....the new emperor sat on a rug as large as a football field, puzzled over conundrums with mathematicians and wallowed in the fantasies of an opium eater."

In the early years of Mughal rule, the capital city was Delhi, not Agra. In 1539 and 1540, Sher Shah, the rebel Afghan, routed Humayun in two decisive battles and became ruler of the Delhi-Agra region. It was in Sher Shah's time that the Grand Trunk Road through Agra was first laid, shaded by trees planted on either side. Humayun recaptured his kingdom in 1555, but died in Delhi soon after, leaving the kingdom in the hands of young Akbar.

Following this confused and troubled period, Agra was to emerge as the Mughal capital, chosen in preference to Delhi, perhaps by an accident of history. The story goes that Delhi fell in Akbar's estimation because of an attempt on his life there.

Not only did Agra become the seat of imperial power, it also became Akbar's spiritual court and a centre for the quest of truth. He received representatives from several religious denominations: black-robed Jesuits, Chinese, Taoist and Confucian scholars, Buddhist monks from Sri Lanka, Sufis and Zoroastrians. Finally, Akbar arrived at what he thought was the quintessence of the religions of the world, Din-i-Ilahi. Akbar's new religion did not outlast him, but it was Akbar's fervour for religious synthesis that led him to Sheikh Salim Chisti, a Sufi mystic, who lived in the village of Sikri, 40 km south-west of Agra.

In 1570, Akbar built the breathtaking city of Fatehpur Sikri as a token of devotion to the saint. Akbar and his court moved to what was probably the most splendid of Mughal capitals. At Fatehpur Sikri could be found some of the most brilliant persons of the time. There was the poet Faizi and his brother Abul Fazl who wrote the sensitive biography of the king, the *Akbar Namah*. There was the witty Birbal and the matchless musician Tansen whose voice, it is said, could set alight a torch. Under Akbar's patronage Surdas and Tulsidas wrote the finest Hindi poetry that is known.

After fifteen years at Fatehpur Sikri, towards the end of his long reign, Akbar took his entourage to the northern borders where he fought a series of battles. Fatehpur Sikri was soon emptied and has remained so till today, a beautiful ghost city. Akbar died in 1605 and was buried at Sikandra, 8 km north-west of Agra. Following Akbar, the thirty-six-year-old Jahangir came to the throne of the vast Mughal empire. He ruled initially from Agra Fort, where he installed a huge bell which could be pulled by a rope by anyone who sought justice from the king.

It was in Jahangir's time that British influence in India began to grow. To his court at Agra came Captain William Hawkins and later Thomas Roe, the ambassador of James I. Roe's journal describes the pomp and splendour, the drinking parties, and the hospitality of Jahangir's court. Tactful and diplomatic, Roe bargained successfully for a *firman* permitting the British to trade at Surat in 1615. In return Jahangir was promised exquisite paintings and embroideries, enamel work and metal statuary from the West.

Shah Jahan, the great Mughal, succeeded Jahangir in the year 1628 and ruled for thirty peaceful years.But in the fourth year of his reign, Shah Jahan was struck by tragedy. After nineteen years of marriage, his beloved wife, the beautiful Mumtaz Mahal, died giving birth to their fourteenth child. The emperor was wild with grief but from the depths of his sorrow he resolved to create the world's greatest monument of love. That was to be the Taj Mahal.

Shah Jahan lacked Akbar's genius but was a capable administrator. He had inherited an overflowing treasury of gold, silver and precious jewels. Drawing from his inexhaustible coffers, he created Mughal India's most lavish extravaganzas. His Peacock Throne of emeralds, diamond and solid silver took seven years to build and cost about twelve million pounds sterling.

*All the emperors contributed to Agra Fort's decorative, marble palaces such as Samman Burj (**top**) and Moti Masjid (**above**). These highly decorative halls vye with some of the private palaces in the scale of their opulence and suggest the life pattern of essentially nomadic kings who liked open spaces, surrounded themselves with gardens, and decorated with a beauty that reflected as much of their aesthetic sensibilities as their love for pomp and splendour. Being smaller, the workmanship at Agra Fort far exceeds the technical excellence of the bigger Red Fort of Delhi.*

And yet Shah Jahan had been educated by the unworldly Sufis. From them he had learnt grammar, logic, mathematics, astronomy and geology. He was well-versed in Arabic, the language of the *Koran*, and in Persian, the language of the court. European travellers have left accounts of the magnificence of Shah Jahan's court which functioned successively from Agra, Lahore and Delhi.

In 1638, Shah Jahan transferred his court to Delhi where he built the Walled City of Shahjahanabad. That marked the end of an era of glory for the city of Agra. Court patronage had given a tremendous impetus to trade and commerce. Agra had become an important textile centre (which it still is), and artisans, bankers, jewellers and merchants from many parts of the country had gathered in the city. It was also a cul-

The Taj Mahal at dusk. The monument is made entirely of marble, and this luminous stone, quarried from Makrana in Rajasthan, takes on a different hue with the changing light of the sun and the moon. It is a presence at dawn that soon turns from the faint flush of pink to a dazzling white, gleaming brilliantly in the afternoon sun, adding patinas of colour in the evening, and glowing with the enchantment of pearls by moonlight.
Preceding pages 46-47: *An overview of Agra Fort which makes it easier to understand why a traveller during Jahangir's reign described the complex 'lyeth in a manner of a half-moon, bellying to the landward'. The river imposed its own defence, and the 70 feet high walls of great solidity that spanned a length of 2.4 km have survived intact for 450 years.*

tural centre with poets, artists and musicians. But towards the end of Shah Jahan's reign, Agra's importance declined. The peasantry and the artisans were in distress. In the latter half of the eighteenth century, the Jats, the Marathas and the Mughals fought for the supremacy of the Agra region. For a time Agra was part of the Gwalior state, ruled by the Scindias. In 1803, when British power was firmly established with the Mughal emperor at Delhi under their protection, Agra too became British territory. From 1833 to 1858 Agra was the capital of the North-West Province.

During the uprising of 1857, when the entire North-West Province was in turmoil, the city of Agra too was convulsed, with British and Indian residents fearing the worst. In July that year the rebel soldiers marched down from Fatehpur Sikri and ripped through the town. As fighting broke out, the Europeans took refuge in Agra Fort.

After British authority was restored and even as the city was returning to normalcy, its population was afflicted by the famine of 1860. During British rule, Agra continued to be an intellectual centre and some of its citizens played an important role in the freedom movement. The British combined Agra and Oudh into the United Provinces of Agra and Oudh; the name was shortened to the United Provinces in 1935. After independence, the United Provinces was renamed Uttar Pradesh. Agra became the headquarters of Agra district, with an area of over 4,800 sq km, and one of the leading cities of India's most populous state.

TAJ MAHAL

IT WAS A ROYAL *MEENA BAZAAR*, colourful, bustling and filled with laughter. The aristocratic women displayed their wares: richly embroidered silks, delicate trinkets, tinkling bells, jewelled mirrors, bangles and beads. Among the women was the unrivalled beauty, Arjumand Banu Begum, the fifteen-year-old daughter of Asaf Khan, the powerful brother-in-law and prime minister of Emperor Jahangir.

The story goes that Jahangir's son, Prince Khurram, struck by the beauty of Arjumand, asked the price of a piece of glass that she had on display. The sprightly girl

retorted teasingly that it was no glass but a diamond and cost Rs. 10,000. The prince picked up the glass, paid without a word and left. He had won the heart of the exquisite Arjumand.

Later, the prince asked of his father a special favour—permission to marry Arjumand. Jahangir raised his right hand to signify his consent. Prince Khurram and Arjumand had to wait five years before they were married and were not even allowed a glimpse of each other during that time.

The marriage of Prince Khurram and Arjumand in 1612 was a spectacular affair. It was at the wedding that Emperor Jahangir gave her the name of Mumtaz Mahal, The Chosen One of the Palace: a name that was to be immortalized in the Taj Mahal. When Prince Khurram fought his way to the throne after his father's death and crowned himself king in 1628, he took the title of Shah Jahan, or King of the World.

Shah Jahan and Mumtaz Mahal led an idyllic life, though the emperor had troubles enough from rebellious nobles. Mumtaz Mahal was his cherished confidant, entrusted with the royal seal, and the emperor's constant companion, even on his military campaigns.

It is said that on her death-bed Mumtaz Mahal had asked Shah Jahan to build an unsurpassed monument in memory of their love, and to fulfill his dying wife's last wish, Shah Jahan set about preparations for the tomb.

Who was the architect who designed the Taj Mahal? Many possibilities have been explored, many theories advanced. But no one really knows. The most commonly accepted name is Ustad Isa. But whether such a person actually existed is a matter of pure conjecture.

The fine, textured marble was brought from the Makrana quarries near Jaipur in Rajasthan; there was jade and crystal from China, turquoise from Tibet, lapis lazuli from Afghanistan, chrysolite from Egypt, agate from Yemen, sapphire from Sri Lanka, amethyst from Persia, coral from Arabia and malachite from Russia. Quartz came from the Himalayas, diamond from the Golconda mines and shell, coral and mother of pearl from the Indian Ocean.

The riches of the world were gathered

A view of the Taj Mahal from Agra Fort. It was such a view that Shah Jahan must have commanded in the last years of his life. Imprisoned by his own son, Aurangzeb, and with only the company of his spinster daughter Jahanara, he led a spartan life under house arrest, looking out to his dying breath at the Taj Mahal, a monument that at one level pleased his senses and at another mocked the very heir he and Mumtaz Mahal had produced.

Overleaf: *Shah Jahan himself must take credit for the design of the Taj Mahal, for though he employed architects, it was essentially his own creation. A verse inscribed by Him on the tomb pays tribute to his own genius : 'The builder could not have been of this earth/ For it is evident the design was given him by heaven'.*

***Right and below:** Details from Shah Jahan's cenotaph. An inkwell is placed above his grave, and in the manner of the Taj itself, it is decorated with agate, lapis lazuli, jade, carnelian, bloodstone and numerous others in floral arabesques. It was an indulgence that Aurangzeb extended to his father on his death. Had Shah Jahan still been the ruler of his dominions when he died, it is possible that he may have ordered the building of a black marble Taj across the Yamuna to house his own mortal remains. Controversy still reigns on whether the foundation for such a structure was ever laid.*

at Agra. There, upon a bend in the river Yamuna, work on the Taj Mahal began. The mausoleum took twenty-two years to build and eventually cost the chief mason his right hand. The earliest foreign visitor to the Taj was the French traveller, Tavernier, who came in the mid-seventeenth century and wrote of the splendour and magnificence of the Taj in his *Travels in India.* Taj Mahal, one of the greatest wonders of the world, cost Shah Jahan five million rupees.

Like the earlier tomb of Humayun at Delhi, the Taj Mahal is set within a square garden. This typical Mughal garden, divided into even squares and intersected by a water channel, and lined by cypresses, has been partially restored today after decades of neglect. On one side of the tomb is the mosque and on the other, the *jawab* (answer). The latter seems to have had no special function other than to provide a visual balance to the mosque.

The main mausoleum stands on a marble platform, with a slender minaret in each corner. These beautiful minarets were deliberately built with a slight outward tilt, so that if they ever collapsed they would fall away from the precious Taj. The pearly white tomb with its gold-topped dome and *pietra dura* inlay contains the octagonal burial chamber, enclosed within a screen of delicately wrought marble. The only asymmetrical element in the whole complex has been contributed by Shah Jahan's son, Aurangzeb, who interred his father beside Mumtaz Mahal to save the trouble and money of building a separate tomb. Mumtaz Mahal's cenotaph has a slate design on it while Shah Jahan's has an ink-pot to signify that the wife should be a slate for the husband to write upon. These cenotaphs are replicas of the real ones which lie in an echoing crypt below. The arches, cornices, walls, passages and the inside of the dome are inlaid with Koranic inscriptions in black marble.

Through the ages the overwhelming beauty of the Taj has received superlative admiration. The French physician Bernier, in his *Travels in the Mughal Empire*, wrote,

> No part can be found that is not skilfully wrought, or that has not its peculiar beauty... Even the squares of white and black marble which compose the pavement are inlaid with these precious stones in the most beautiful and delightful manner imaginable.

A 19th century administrator, Col. W.H. Sleeman, in his *Rambles and Recollections of an Indian official*, in 1844:

> For five and twenty years of my life had I been looking forward to the sight now before me. Of no building on earth had I heard so much as of this, which contains the remains of the Emperor Shah Jahan and his wife... and from the first sight of the dome and minarets on the distant horizon, to the last glance back from my tent-ropes to the magnificent gateway that forms the entrance from our camp to the quadrangle in which

they stand, I can truly say that everything surpassed my expectations. I at first thought the dome formed too large a portion of the whole building; that its neck was too long and too much exposed; and that the minarets were too plain in their design; but after going repeatedly over every part, and examining the *tout ensemble* from all possible positions, and in all possible lights, from that of the full moon at midnight in a cloudless sky, to that of the noon-day sun, the mind seemed to repose in the calm persuasion that there was an entire harmony of parts, a faultless congregation of architectural beauties, on which it could dwell forever without fatigue.

I went on from part to part in the expectation that I must by-and-by come to something that would disappoint me; but no, the emotion which one feels at first is never impaired: on the contrary, it goes on improving from the first *coup d'oeil* of the dome in the distance, to the minute inspection of the last flower upon the screen around the tomb. One returns and returns to it with undiminished pleasure which he derives from the contemplation of the greater, and of the whole collectively, seems to increase; and he leaves it with a feeling of regret, that he could not have it all his life within his reach; and of the assurance that the image of what he has seen can never be obliterated from his mind...

A few decades later, Rudyard Kipling, wrote of the Taj as seen by a tourist thus:

...then as the train sped forward, and the mists shifted and the sun shone upon the mists, the Taj took a hundred new shapes, each perfect and each beyond description. It was the Ivory Gate through which all dreams come true... it seemed the embodiment of all things pure, all things holy and all things unhappy. That was the mystery of the building. It may be that the mists wrought the witchery, and that the Taj seen in the dry sunlight is only, as guidebooks say, a noble structure. The Englishman could not tell, and has made a vow that he will never go nearer the spot, for fear of breaking the charm of the unearthy pavilions.

It may be, too, that each must view the Taj for himself, with his own eyes, working out his own interpretation of the sight. It is certain that no man can in cold blood and colder ink set down 'his impressions if he has been in the least moved. To the one who watched and wondered that November morning the thing seemed full of sorrow — the sorrow of the man who built it for the woman he loved, and the sorrow of the workmen who died in the building, used up like cattle. And in the face of this sorrow the Taj flushed in the sunlight and was beautiful, after the beauty of a woman who has done no wrong.

Top and left: *Details of carvings on sandstone from the mosque in the Taj Mahal complex. The consummate artistry of the builders combined the Hindu love for decoration with the Persianised designs to create an effect that was rich. The sandstone walls used lighter coloured stones for relief when forming borders for sections that were carved so realistically that the subject appeared natural.*
Overleaf: *A view of the cenotaphs in the lower hall where the graves of Shah Jahan and Mumtaz Mahal receive the homage of thousands of visitors daily, the sombre room fittingly lit by one overhead light. Mumtaz's grave is in the centre of the hall, that of Shah Jahan, though larger, off centre, the only assymetrical structure in a building that excels in the purity of its proportions. The marble screen that surrounds their graves replaced an earlier gold railing that was temporarily erected to girdle Mumtaz's grave. Shah Jahan's grave is inscribed with all his titles, that of Mumtaz with the 99 names of God.*

And finally there came Lord Curzon who said, in a speech he gave from one of the terraces of this noble building:

The central dome of the Taj rises like some vast exhalation into the thin air, and on the other side the red rampart of the Fort stands like a crimson barricade against the sky...If I had never done anything else in

Like Delhi, Agra has its share of tombs, but there is none so beautiful as Sikandra. Started by Akbar himself, its open pyramidal structure had some mystical significance, and was completed by Jahangir. ***Preceding pages 56-57:*** *The sandstone gateway to the Taj Mahal is decorated with marble tiles and inlaid with motifs in a continuation of the style of the Taj itself. The rich red colour offsets the luminiscence of the mausoleum itself.*

India, I have written my name here, and the letters are a living joy.

It has been described as "a tender elegy in marble", "a lustrous pearl". The French novelist Pierre Loti wrote, "The wonder of wonders is the white grill that stands in the centre of the translucent hall and encloses the tomb of the sultana. It is made of plaques of marble placed upright, so finely worked that it might be thought that they were carved in ivory...little garlands of tulips, fuchsias, and immortelles are worked in mosaics of turquoise, topaz, porphyry or lapiz lazuli. The sonority of this white mausoleum is almost terrifying, for the echoes never seem to cease."

Shah Jahan lived eight long years in confinement, looking out through a window at the beautiful Taj Mahal. As he lay dying at the age of 74, a tiny mirror was embedded at an angle in the wall next to his bed, so that he could gaze at the image of his cherished wife's tomb. It is said that when he died, he was found with his head turned towards that little mirror.

A fitting epitaph for Shah Jahan, and a tribute to the Taj was penned by the poet Rabindranath Tagore:

> You knew, Shah Jahan, life and youth, wealth and glory, they all drift away in the current of time. You strove, therefore, to perpetuate only the sorrow of your heart. Kingly power, stern as thunder, may sink into sleep like the glowing embers of the setting sun...Let the splendour of diamond, pearl and ruby vanish like the magic shimmer of the rainbow. Only let this one teardrop, this Taj Mahal, glisten spotlessly bright on the cheek of time, forever and ever.

Today the Taj faces another threat: atmospheric pollution. In 1979, after having spent five years and nearly Rs. 7 million on assessing the air pollution threat to the Taj Mahal, the Indian government decided that the 300-year-old monument would not be endangered by the sulphur dioxide emissions of the new six million tonne oil refinery set up near Mathura, 40 km north-west of Agra. Indian and foreign experts have found the marble of the Taj "well preserved" but have said that the sandstone monuments of Agra are showing signs of decay.

The colonnaded arcades of Diwan i Khas, the hall of public audience at Agra Fort. It was here the emperors would spend their mornings, dealing with issues of public litigation, the supplicants gathering in these lofty chambers to meet their ruler. Carpets covered their floors, and awnings and curtains draped the pillars; communion with the people was better established in these royal surroundings without walls acting as a restrictive barrier.

FATEHPUR SIKRI

THE SEED OF A SAINT'S BLESSING gave Akbar a child by a Hindu wife in the year 1569. This happy circumstance, and the comparative stability afforded by the 1560s, inspired Akbar to begin work on the building of a city dedicated to the beneficent Sufi saint, Salim Chisti, in one of the earliest experiments in the marriage of Hindu and Muslim architectural styles, which was later to flower into the magnificent productions of the Indo-Islamic school. This city was Fatehpur Sikri, 40 km south-west of Agra, where Akbar based himself for fifteen years or so, until the demands of imperial defence forced him back to his usual peripatetic mode.

By a curious historical coincidence, Akbar's new city was located at the very site where his grandfather, Babar, had regrouped his forces after defeating Ibrahim Lodi, and where he had caused a garden to be laid out. Akbar's reason for selecting this site was, however, different: Sikri was the place where Salim Chisti was based, and his beautiful marble tomb, where barren women still go in the hope of gaining divinely-ordained fertility, still stands amidst the ruins of Sikri.

The construction of Fatehpur Sikri had begun, however, with the building of the Jama Masjid, around which the rest of the city was later constructed. The *masjid* which faces Mecca, in accordance with Islamic prescriptions, gives the city its axial orientation, according to which the other, and later, buildings are set out.

In addition to the imposing Jama Masjid and Salim Chisti's tomb, Fatehpur Sikri houses other buildings of great architectural interest: the Diwan-i-Am, where Akbar used to give audience to the common people; the Diwan-i-Khas, dominated by a massive throne that seems almost to be suspended from above; Rani Jodhabai's palace, with its melange of regional architectural styles; the eccentrically named Turkish Sultana's residence, a delicately decorated pavilion located in the male quarters, which probably functioned as some kind of a discussion room; Mariam's Palace, Akbar's mother's residence, with its severe exterior, but exquisite interior decor;

The highlight of the Panchmahal complex of five storeys (the actual palace cannot be seen in this picture) is the Anup Talao, a waterbody that gave the whole structure an airy, light feeling emphasised in the delicate quality of the construction.
Facing page: *The interior of Fatehpur Sikri's Diwan i Khas focuses on this richly carved pillar with its dense carvings of brackets arranged in a circular arrangement.*
Overleaf: *An overview of Fatehpur Sikri, the grand city planned by Akbar in thanksgiving for the birth of an heir but which he had to abandon soon after for it lacked adequate water reservoirs.*

the upwardly-tapering Panch Mahal with its 176 columns which present an extraordinary variety, and where Akbar spent time with only his most favourite consorts; the Hawa Mahal, where Akbar caught the breeze in the hot summer months; the Anup Talao; and the magnificent doorways, of which the most celebrated is the Buland Darwaza, which was built to commemorate Akbar's conquest of Gujarat. It would be difficult anywhere in the world to find such a profusion and variety of architectural artifices in an area of the same size.

Akbar's city was unusual for the times in that it was a planned city—laid out in modules that followed the injunctions of sacred Islamic proportions, and was inspired by the settlement pattern of the camps that the wandering Mughal courts were wont so effortlessly to put up in the course of their campaigns and other peregrinations. It thus consisted of four enclosures—the first one for royal interactions with the hoi polloi; the second for nobles; the third for the emperor to relax in; and the innermost one, protected by eunuchs with the utmost of zeal, for the royal harem.

There is nothing haphazard about the architectural conception of Fatehpur, and the minute attention to detail that it evinces leaves one in no doubt that an architectural genius must have guided its planning. Look at the way that the working quarters had been laid out in relation to the residential quarters. The kitchens and baths were, for instance, located below the ridge around which the city was built, while the palaces were located high on the ridge. This facilitated the movement of services to the central node of consumption, and made organization a much easier matter.

In counterpoint to this rigidity was the openness of the setting. Sikri, unlike most medieval cities, was not walled in, nor was its citadel fortified. This, and its relatively unostentatious architectural style, gave it an ambience of relaxed informality which is Sikri's particular contribution to Indo-Islamic architecture.

It was in Fatehpur Sikri that Akbar assembled a glittering array of scholars, poets, musicians, statesmen and theologians who typified the liberal and enquiring spirit

The most significant aspect of Sikandra, Akbar's tomb, is the use of mosaics and inlays as a decorative theme. While no doubt ordered according to the architectural pattern as established by Akbar, it was Jehangir who is responsible for the mausoleums's striking pattern. Work on the tomb had been on for a few years before Jehangir visited the site, and was appalled by what he saw. Changes were immediately ordered, but though little could be done about the physical structure, he ensured the use of marble, of decorative inlay, planned the elaborate southern gateway and conceived a garden in the formal quadrangle with an irrigation system that has remained effective to the day. The fifth floor with its girdling of marble was intentionally left open so that during Akbar's Urs a 'rich tent' could cover the tomb.

of his reign. It was in Fatehpur Sikri that Akbar discussed religion with the representatives of the major religions of the world, and formulated his eclectic though somewhat esoteric and exclusive religion, the Din-i-Ilahi. It was in Sikri again that Akbar, who was illiterate, sat in his sumptuously decorated library to hear scholars read out a wide range of literature to him.

At a less sublime level, in the palace courtyard was played the game of *pachisi*, a sort of medieval Indian equivalent of chess. The uniqueness of these games, popular myth would have us believe, was that they were played with live human pieces.

Ultimately, however, Fatehpur Sikri had to be abandoned due to the combination of a number of factors. Chief among these were, probably, a lack of water, unassuaged even by the ingeniously designed network of aqueducts that carried water from a central reservoir constructed in such a manner that it trapped all the available water, and the need for Akbar's presence at the threatened north-western borders. After the court abandoned Sikri, it fell into disuse and became a ghost town. Time and the ineluctable forces of nature have wreaked their wonted havoc on Sikri. Much has been lost. But from what remains, the beauty and enchantment of Akbar's 'city of victory' can be divined and felt, even if no more recaptured.

HERITAGE

WHEN AKBAR DIED HE WAS BURIED at Sikandra, 10 km north-west of Agra. This tomb, built in 1613, is an architectural regression, far less pleasing than that of Humayun built earlier at Delhi. The truncated pyramidal tomb is set in a square garden. Its decorative gateway with bold inlay work is topped by four marble minarets which appear here for the first time in India.

The only significant piece of architecture of Jahangir's time is the tomb of his father-in-law, the Itmad-ud-Daulah, or the Pillar of the State. "This is Agra's other great wonder. If stones could speak they would tell you that the serene resting place of Itmad-ud-Daulah tells of the love of a great Mughal emperor for a ravishingly beautiful woman. Mehr-un-Nisa was the daughter of Itmad-ud-Daulah. One story goes that she captivated Emperor Jahangir at the annual fair at which court ladies set up stalls where, in an atmosphere of gaiety and flirtation, the emperor went shopping. He married her, called her Nur Jahan, or Light of the World, and raised her father to the highest ministerial position in his court, a position he held all his life. When her father died, Nur Jahan built a mausoleum in his memory. Here craftsmen have surpassed themselves with a profusion of intricate *chikan*-work, translucent marble screens, and have experimented for the first time with *pietra dura* inlay, a technique to be used later in the Taj Mahal."

There is another monumental Mughal building in Agra which the visitor cannot miss. This is the massive red sandstone Agra Fort. The semicircular fort on the river bank was one of Akbar's earliest building projects, started in 1565, though completed only in 1574, and later drastically altered by Shah Jahan. The 20 metre high masonry walls were so solid that, it is said, a hair could not find its way into the joints.

The Jahangir Mahal, with an elaborately carved façade and green and blue tiling on the upper storey, is reminiscent of Hindu palaces. This is one of the few structures of Akbar's time which has survived within the fort, though the *Ain-i-Akbari* mentions 500 edifices.These were probably demolished by Shah Jahan who preferred marble to sandstone. He rebuilt and expanded the Diwan-i-Am and the Diwan-i-Khas and built the delicate Pearl Mosque or Moti Masjid in 1654. This white marble mosque has a black inscription over its doorway and yellow marble inlaid in the floor. It is topped by three small domes and a row of kiosks.

Like the Lal Qila at Delhi, the Agra Fort has seen both grand and tumultuous times. In 1657, when Shah Jahan fell ill and the struggle for succession broke out among his sons, Aurangzeb entered the city of Agra and forced his father to surrender the fort by cutting off the water supply from the Yamuna. Shah Jahan lived out his life as a captive in the fort, consoled by his favourite daughter Jahanara and taking solace in the *Koran* and the sight of the beautiful Taj Mahal which he could see through his window.

In architecture, Muslim design and Hindu stonemasonry had combined to evolve a unique style under the Mughals. So too in painting. The amalgam of the two sometimes contradictory traditions developed into a rich and vigorous style in Akbar's time. Indian painting may at first appear contradictory, influenced at different periods by various foreign cultures, but as Archer says, "we can only ascribe its national character to the overriding stimulus of India itself." The two main styles of indigenous painting had been the supple naturalism of the Ajanta murals and the bold distortion of the Jain miniatures. The Muslims too had the highly formalized school of Tabriz and the more fluid style of Meshed.

Some of the best paintings and illustrated manuscripts in this school were developed under Akbar. Finely polished paper, decorative margins, golden landscapes of animals and flowers and exquisite calligraphy were used. The *Akbar Namah* portrays events from the emperor's life, a kind of historical narrative. In the time of Jahangir, portrait painting reached its zenith and the first ceremonial elements appeared. By the time of Shah Jahan a more stylized treatment developed.

The realistic animal and bird paintings of Jahangir's time influenced the minor arts too. Mughal textiles, their silks and brocades, had floral motifs and natural landscapes rather like a painting. Their pictorial carpets and rugs in luxuriant colours were distinctive and unlike anything outside Mughal India.

Agra is still an important carpet-producing centre. Its green, blue and fawn carpets have a cotton base; the designs have come down from Mughal times. Agra also produces striped cotton *durries* or rugs. Like Delhi, Agra too is well-known for its silk embroideries. Today, a variety of household materials, such as cushion covers and curtains, are embroidered in coloured silk, in quilted, satin-stitch designs.

In Mughal times there was a wealth of minor arts in Agra: jade carvings with delicate floral motifs or precious metal objects, such as mirrors or dagger handles, encrusted with jewels or gold wire. The art of damascening, or *koftgari*, in which one metal is encrusted in the form of a wire into another, fascinated Emperor Akbar who is supposed to have supervised this work in his armoury himself. Agra is no longer an important centre of metal craft but the intricate *jali* work in stone and marble is still done. The *jali* of filigreed marble or fretted sandstone may have a network of floral or geometrical designs or both. Various decorative articles like plates, vases, candlesticks are made of marble inlaid with coloured stones. At Fatehpur Sikri, soapstone models and ornamental objects are made largely for the tourist market.

Today, Agra is known for its leather craft which has developed into a major industry. The majority of the shoemaking factories in Uttar Pradesh are located at Agra. The shoes are handmade in Agra's lanes and bylanes from locally available hides and skins.

With its rich heritage, Agra is one of India's greatest tourist centres.

The façade of Itmad-ud-Daulah, the riverside tomb of Mirza Ghyas Beg, Nur Jahan's father, reveals the love for ornamentation which had made its mark in the architecture of Jehangir's reign. If the structure lacks spatial elegance on account of its short minarets, it serves in turn to highlight the inlay which is such an important aspect of the tomb's decoration, skilfully blending sandstone with different shades of marble and jasper. More significant than the physical structure of the building is its connotation: Ghyas Beg had arrived penniless in Agra from Persia, and it was only after the emperor chose his widowed daughter of 34 years as his bride that he was appointed prime minister.

Overleaf: *A rare aerial view of the Taj Mahal. Shah Jahan, who considered himself a great builder, built a memorial that took 22 years in the making, employed a workforce of 20,000, and was set in a garden in the manner of a place of pilgrimage to the shrine of a martyr as one who had died in childbirth is considered by the Muslim fraternity.*

The Great Mughals

IN 1526, BABAR, LEADER OF A Central Asian tribe, descendant of Taimur and Chenghiz Khan, frustrated in his attempt to secure Samarqand, his inheritance, came to the Indian sub-continent where he defeated Ibrahim Lodi, the Afghan Sultan of Delhi, at the strategic battlefield of Panipat, and established a tenuous toe-hold in the region. From this beginning was to grow the magnificent edifice of the Mughal empire which, at its apogee, was to stretch from the north-western reaches of Kabul and Kandahar to the heart of the Deccan plateau in the southern part of the sub-continent. The glorious days of this empire were to span the rule of four emperors, from 1556 to 1707, after which it began a precipitous and spectacular decline that was to culminate, in 1857, in the crowning of the British Queen, Victoria, as Empress of India.

Babar was soon forced to defend his newly-won acquisition. But a victory over the forces of Rana Sanga of Malwa at Khanwa put the issue temporarily beyond doubt. Babar was not destined, however, to enjoy for long the fruits of his martial labours. He died in 1530. Legend has it that when Humayun, the heir-apparent, was seriously ill, Babar circled the young prince's bed nine times and wished upon himself his son's illness. His death may have been providential for the future of the fledgling empire since he had not evinced, in his few years in India, an administrative acumen that could even begin to match his martial prowess.

Babar's death brought to the throne his son Humayun. The scholarly and aesthetically-inclined Humayun inherited a kingdom that had virtually no administrative framework and was beset on all sides by antagonists—Afghans, Rajputs—intent on wresting for themselves the throne of Delhi. Of these the most redoubtable was a petty Afghan chieftain whose vaulting ambition was matched by a multi-faceted genius. Sher Shah Suri not only succeeded in winning Humayun's dominions from him, but in the short span of four years evolved the embryo of an administrative and communications network that was to become the blueprint for Akbar's later imperial consolidation. But Sher Shah too met an untimely death. He died while besieging the fort of Kalinjar in an accidental gunpowder blast. His death gave Humayun just the breathing space he needed, and he was soon able to recover his kingdom. Like his father before him, however, his enjoyment of kingship too was short-lived. A fall down the steep stairways that led to his much-loved library brought an end to his life.

Akbar

Jahangir

Thus, in 1555, came to the shaky throne of Delhi the 13-year-old son of Humayun, the emperor Akbar. When Akbar ascended the throne his guardian Bairam Khan ruled in his stead as regent. In the next year, in another battle at the same strategic battlefield of Panipat, Bairam Khan engineered a signal triumph over the pretender Hemu and for the first time set Babar's empire on a firmer footing.

Akbar exiled his mentor, Bairam Khan, who was later murdered by a fanatic. Akbar subsequently set about the task of expanding the kingdom he had inherited, and giving to it a coherent administrative basis. Akbar, who ruled till his death in 1605, was successful in expanding his dominions to Bengal in the east and Rajputana in the west. At the end of his reign, the Mughal empire, for by then it certainly merited this description, stretched from Kandahar to the Deccan Plateau, and from the Bay of Bengal to the Arabian Sea.

Akbar achieved all this by a judicious blend of diplomacy and war. In Rajputana he bought the loyalty of a number of Rajput chieftains, and their recognition of his suzerainty, by setting up an intricate network of marital alliances, and by making free with the privileged feudal rights that came to be known as *watan jagirs.* But against those chieftains who refused to succumb to his blandishments, as, for instance, did Rana Pratap, he waged war relentlessly. Even the indubitably valiant and tenacious Rana Pratap was subdued by Akbar's superior firepower.

Akbar's more seminal contribution lay, however, in his establishment of an administrative framework that brought relative peace, tranquillity and order to his empire, and made possible the efflorescence of art, architecture, music and literature that characterized his rule and those of his immediate successors. In his court at Fatehpur Sikri he assembled a galaxy of artistes among whom numbered the matchless musician Tansen, the chronicler Abul Fazl, and his brother, the poet Faizi. The administration functioned through the *mansabdari* and *jagirdari* systems under which civil and military servants of the empire were allocated clearly defined duties and status in accordance with which they were remunerated by the revenues of land grants (*jagirs*) which were subject to transfer. This system had the great virtue, from the emperor's point of view, of not allowing individual nobles to build bases of power, and thus helped to centralize power in the hands of the imperial household.

Nur Jahan's niece, whose beauty has gone down in legend, at a fair, and, after receiving parental approval, married her. Jahangir, Shah Jahan's father, named her Mumtaz Mahal, the chosen one of the palace. It was as a requiem to her memory that Shah Jahan had the Taj Mahal built. One of the wonders of the world, the Taj Mahal took twenty-two years in the making, and the materials for its construction came from all over the world. But its exquisite, breathtaking beauty more than justifies the lavish expenditure of time and money. Akbar had begun the Mughal tradition of building. Jahangir continued it, but the apogee of Mughal architecture was reached under the patronage of Shah Jahan, whose legacy includes such treasures as the Red Fort and the Agra Fort.

vicious spiral of exploitation of both natural resources and subjects, provoking widespread agrarian resistance that contributed most significantly to the disintegration of the empire. Ambitious contestants, namely the Maratha leader, Shivaji, and his successors, drew upon this agrarian discontent to plague Aurangzeb and his descendants. Historians, on the whole, have been unkind to Aurangzeb. He is remembered as a bigot and a fanatic, even though many Hindu noblemen, including Jai Singh, who had destroyed innumerable mosques, rose to prominence in imperial service in his reign. Few remember, too, that Aurangzeb's personal expenses were met not from the treasures of the imperial coffers, but from what he earned selling caps which he used to make with his own hands.

Nur Jahan

Mumtaz Mahal

Shah Jahan

The two succeeding emperors, Jahangir and Shah Jahan, have gone down in history for their fairy-tale romances and architectural achievements. Legend has it that Jahangir fell in love with and married Mehr-un-nisa, the exquisitely beautiful wife of Sher Afghan, the *subahdar* of Bengal. Jahangir christened her Nur Jahan, the light of the world. Nur Jehan soon became the real power behind the throne, a perfect counterbalance to Jahangir's temperamental inaptitude for the exacting task of imperial governance. Her father rose to prominence in Jahangir's court, and came to be known as Itmad-ud-Daulah, the pillar of the state.

Shah Jahan met Arjumand Begum,

One of Shah Jahan's sons, Aurangzeb, came to the throne following a bitter war of succession while his father was still alive. Shah Jahan lived out his last years imprisoned in the Agra Fort by his son, but solaced by the presence of his favourite daughter, the bold and outspoken Jahanara, and the constant sight of his beloved Mumtaz's mausoleum, the Taj Mahal. Aurangzeb's ambitious project of extending the frontiers of the empire further, deep into the Deccan Plateau, though temporarily successful was ultimately responsible for the downfall of the empire. In trying to conquer the Deccan, Aurangzeb stretched the resources of the empire beyond breaking point. This triggered off a

That Aurangzeb was followed by inefficient and effete rulers, with such examples as the poet-emperor Bahadur Shah Zafar, who couldn't exercise any control over their court and nobility, did little to help the imperial cause. Ambitious, territorial governors broke away to form successor states—as in Bengal, Hyderabad and Awadh; and coteries gained control of the court, most notably in the case of the egregious Saiyyid brothers, styled by latter-day historians as 'the kingmakers'. Foreign invaders despoiled the empire, internal antagonists, like the Marathas held it to ransom, and it was left to the last of the conquerors, the British imperialists, to deliver the *coup de grace* in 1857.

JAIPUR

The Citadel of Victory

There is a popular saying in Jaipur that to be a man one must know how to wield the sword, the pen and the brush. As a city, Jaipur, barely 250 year old, exhibits just this versatility in its palaces and profusion of handicrafts, its poetry, music and literature, its palaces and its rugged forts.

Jaipur is one of India's loveliest cities. It has a living, vital quality that arises from a coexistence of diverse factors — aristocratic elegance and vibrant folk traditions; a growing, spacious city and crowded old bazaars; industrialization and craftsmen carrying on the skill of generations; plush, streamlined houses and palaces and forts that seem to belong more to the world of fairy tales; camel carts and *ekkas* and speeding sports cars; the polo-playing elite and the simple peasants from the desert.

Linked to Mughal India by sheer proximity and the forces of history, the proud people of Jaipur retained a measure of independence even while absorbing much of Mughal culture. In British times the rose-pink city, like most of Rajasthan, was somewhat isolated from the rest of India though it continued to flourish as a commercial and cultural centre. Today, as the capital of the sprawling state of Rajasthan, Jaipur is still growing. And it still has a very definite character of its own.

Three hundred kilometres south-west of Delhi, Jaipur is in the east of the Rajasthan plain. To its north and west are dune and scrub and the land is sandy and barren; to its south and east it gradually gives way to a greater proportion of cultivated green. Once the rains come, the hills surrounding Jaipur turn green. The plateau south-east of Jaipur is drained by the Chambal river and its tributaries. It is volcanic in origin, a wide stony upland with occasional tracts of deep black soil (the remains of black lava and alluvial loam) in the river valleys. The local name for this region has long been *pathar* or stone. The broken chain of hills towards the north and west of Jaipur are an offshoot of the Aravalli range, beyond which lies the great Rajasthan desert.

The presence of the desert is an undercurrent in Jaipur: in its camel carts and snake charmers, its *shehnai* players and puppeteers, its peasant women in swirling skirts and anklets, its menfolk with their curling moustaches and their proudly tied turbans. It is known by its sobriquet, the 'Pink City', but the life of its people is etched in warm, earthy colours which reflect their innate love for beauty and colour.

HISTORY

"YOUR ANCESTORS GAVE ME MUCH trouble. Now say what you deserve of me before saying what you desire," said the Mughal Emperor Aurangzeb to the young Rajput lad, barely eleven years old, who had just succeeded to the throne of Amber. The boy was stunned for a moment as the

Facing page: *Enroute to Jaipur from Delhi, a short detour takes one to Samode Palace, an exquisite fortified settlement in the Aravalli hills. This was one of the feudal states that owed allegiance to Jaipur, and its head was once the state's prime minister. A Kalbeliya dancer and her troupe of dancers are framed at an opportune moment at the entrance to the palace.*
This page: *Colourful puppets are a distinctive feature of Jaipur. Visitors will see them in shops, or at puppet shows arranged for them at their hotels.*

This page and opposite: Jaipur is just over 250 years old, yet it has a tremendous historical presence. In the walled city, the humblest homes and shops are brightened through the use of sensitive architecture juxtaposed with traditional paintings. When it was being built, the city's architect, Vidyadhar, ensured that all building plans were first approved by him before being cleared for construction, one of the reasons why the old city has developed so harmoniously.*

Emperor grasped his hands in one of his own and mocked: "Tell me what use your arms are now?"

Upon this, the child king retorted swiftly: "Your Majesty, when a bridegroom takes his bride's hand in one of his own during the wedding, he is bound by duty to protect her all his life. Now that the Emperor of India has taken my hands in his right hand, what have I to fear? With your Majesty's long arms to protect me,

what other arms do I need?"

The Emperor, whose bigoted principles and policies had antagonized the Rajputs, was overwhelmed by the boy's tact and presence of mind. And thus, for his quick repartee, the boy Jai Singh earned the title of *Sawai* (literally, 'one-and-a-quarter') from the Emperor; Aurangzeb predicted that he would measure a quarter above the other rajahs.

Eventually, of course, Jai Singh was to rank much taller than that — as one of the most illustrious Rajput rulers. He extended the state of Amber several times beyond its original size and shifted its capital to the plains, where he built a brand new city, Jaipur.

After Aurangzeb's death, the Mughal empire began gradually to go to seed. A succession of weak rulers lost control not only over the empire, but also over their own court. The atmosphere at the court was vitiated by intrigue and factional rivalries. Sawai Jai Singh found himself unable to remain in the Mughal court in such circumstances. He left and went back to his native state and devoted himself to the construction and completion of his new capital. Jaipur took seven years in the making — it was begun in 1720 and completed in 1727.

The new capital prospered. The eighteenth century was a turbulent period for northern India, and with the Delhi-Agra-Mathura region open to attack from the Mughal marauders in the north and the Marathas from the south, Jaipur became a haven for traders. Moneylenders and jewellers from Agra and Delhi converged here to make it a centre for jewellery, banking and industry.

The Kachwaha clan of Rajputs, to which Sawai Jai Singh II belonged, traced their descent from the sun itself. Archaeological evidence points to Mauryan settlements in the Jaipur-Amber area in the fourth century BC. Amber itself was perhaps founded in the tenth century and by the twelfth century, the Kachwahas had firmly established themselves in the area.

Unlike other Rajput states such as Udaipur, the house of Amber was never a great adversary of the Mughal rulers in Delhi. In the sixteenth century, Bahar Mal had received a 5,000 horse command from Humayun. To seal the pact of friendship, Bahar Mal gave his daughter in marriage to Emperor Akbar, Humayun's son and successor. Bahar Mal's son had a high position in Akbar's court and his grandson, Man Singh, was the commander-in-chief of Akbar's forces. No wonder the House of Amber figures prominently in the chronicle of Akbar's reign, the *Ain-i-Akbari.*

Jaipur derives its name from its illustrious ruler (*jai* means victory). The city was one of the best planned in India. The original plan still exists, and it bears a strong resemblance to the grid pattern of modern cities in the West. It was divided into nine squares, separated by wide roads. The City Palace and its gardens were at the centre. Along the main streets were the bazaars, built with remarkable uniformity. Above the bazaars lived the city dwellers, who entered their homes through bylanes that branched off the main roads. Every type of craftsmen was allotted a particular locality, and today their descendants, who continue to practise the same craft, still live in the same localities. The old city, most of which is still intact, is surrounded by high walls, and can be entered through eight magnificent gateways. Today, though Jaipur has spread far beyond, the old walled city remains its nerve centre, and its most colourful area.

Sawai Jai Singh was a man of many parts — soldier, statesman, scholar, builder, astronomer and master diplomat. He concluded an alliance with the Maharana of Udaipur, a long-standing adversary; in keeping with the custom of the period, Jai Singh sealed the agreement with the Maharana by marrying his daughter. In return for Udaipur's military and political support, Jai Singh promised that the son born of this alliance would be the heir to his throne. He also assured his new queen several privileges: her palanquin would be the foremost in a procession, she would be accorded the most respect in the *zenana* (the women's palace), and her husband would spend all festival nights with her. These were among the points actually set down as part of the treaty.

The Jaipur ruler had something of a matrimonial record among Rajput kings. He had twenty-eight wives and four concubines. Inevitably, after his death there was a battle for succession, notwithstanding the treaty with Udaipur. In the confusion that followed, Jaipur lost some of its territory and much of its prestige as it was successively attacked by the Marathas and the Jats.

Relations with the other Rajput states, too, were indifferent. However, for a time, three major Rajput states — Mewar, Marwar, and Amber or Jaipur — joined forces to attack Bahadur Shah I, a descendant of Aurangzeb. But they were not successful.

The eighteenth century thus saw the decline of Rajputana's individual kingdoms. The quarrels over succession made these states vulnerable to attacks from the Marathas and Muslims. Anarchy, plunder and economic ruin followed. In Tod's language, it "ended only with the total ruin and humiliation of this noble race".

In the meantime, the British had begun to rapidly expand their dominion over the rest of the country. Like the Mughals before them, they were quick to grasp the importance of having the Rajputs as allies, and opened negotiations with some of the Rajput states.

The anarchy following the Maratha raids and their own internal dissensions had paved the way for British supremacy

Overleaf: *The fort of Nahargarh which provides the best bird's eye-view of the city's modern sprawl. Built by the maharaja as a retreat for his zenana, it is easy to imagine the royal women promenading on these fortifications as they looked towards their beloved city in the blistering summer months.*

A steep, curving path leads to the ramparts of Amber, the fortified city that was home to the Kachwaha Rajputs before they shifted their capital to Jaipur. Visitors today wend their way up the steep slopes on elephant-back in a manner reminiscent of royal processions—for a moment it is easy to believe yourself a maharaja!

in Rajputana. After that, it was a matter of time before these once fiercely independent states entered into defensive alliances with the British. Between 1817 and 1823, Kotah, Udaipur, Bundi, Kishangarh, Bikaner, Jaisalmer and Jaipur all signed such treaties, bartering away their independence for British protection.

In the early nineteenth century, Delhi and Agra came under British rule. In a few years, British sway extended to Jaipur, and by 1818 they were completely in control. Maharaja Jagat Singh concluded a treaty with the British Resident, Sir Charles Metcalfe. Unlike the rulers of Delhi and Agra, the Jaipur rulers remained loyal to the British during the 1857 uprising.

With the departure of the British in 1947, the rulers of the princely states, including those of Rajputana, acceded to the Indian Union. In compensation the four largest Rajput states, Bikaner, Jaipur, Jodhpur and Jaisalmer were merged, and finally, in 1956, the state of Rajasthan, as it exists today, came into being with Jaipur as its capital. For the loss of their kingdoms or what remained of them, they received privy purses, but the former rulers were well and truly reduced to ordinary citizens. A book on the subject records that some Maharajas, faced with sudden impoverishment, were reduced to selling family heirlooms. But they kept their palaces and many of them judiciously proceeded to convert them into luxury hotels. Udaipur, Jodhpur, Jaipur, Bharatpur and Bikaner all offer these palace hotels. The House of Jaipur is believed to have been the wealthiest as well as the most well-ordered of the princely families in Rajasthan. Its scions have gone into business and industry.

HERITAGE

THE RAJPUTS WERE GREAT BUILDERS, and when they borrowed ideas they did so tastefully. The House of Jaipur's close historical association with the Mughals is evident in the architecture of its first capital, Amber, where the earliest extant buildings date to the sixteenth century. Many of them were constructed during the reign of Maharaja Man Singh (1592-1615), and Raja Jai Singh made major addi-

The sprawling palaces of Amber are contained within fortifications that merge into the hillside to offer defence. The former capital was a city that rivalled Akbar's Fatehpur Sikri and was once described to the Mughal as 'tier upon tier of beautiful buildings'. The Rajputs had reason to believe their city would seize the Mughals with envy, and when a visit by Akbar was anticipated, the maharaja had one of the most exquisite palaces covered with stucco to hide the decorations.

tions before he died in 1668. Amber Fort has within its walls old and new palaces, the latter built by Maharaja Man Singh and Raja Jai Singh II. The old palaces are as stark as the new are opulent.

The profusion of fortresses, in one sense, is an indication of the times, for frequent invasions and counter-invasions marked attempts at territorial expansion. Forts were built to hold down the conquered country and to keep the people in subjugation, as well as to protect and secure a town against invaders.

Architects of the period have described the principles on which the fortresses were generally planned. For the safety of the inhabitants, these were to be constructed on an eminence, protected by bastions and gates, and guarded by armed forces. They were to be amply provided with wells, tanks, pools, as well as agricultural land, so as to be able to hold out during long sieges. Walls were constructed in several concentric rows, and wide moats dug.

Nestled in a pass in a rocky gorge around a lake and protected by the fortresses on the ridge above, Amber Fort is a picturesque sight. A long, winding ramp leads to an imposing gateway which opens on to a courtyard that provides access to Sawai Jai Singh's palaces. The Diwan-i-Am is distinctly Mughal in style and was perhaps built by masons who had been trained by Akbar's supervisors.

Facing the Diwan-i-Am is a huge doorway, the Ganesh Pol. It is the entrance to the palaces and its painted façade is considered more Hindu than Muslim in style. The builders were able to harmonize the two styles by an ingenious set of arcades. Beyond the courtyard are several palaces, *zenana* apartments, terraces, gardens — a rich complex of buildings which rival even Akbar's Fatehpur Sikri. The Rajputs also picked up the art of inlaid mirror work from the Mughals. The palaces in Jaipur and Udaipur have borrowed the idea of a Sheesh Mahal, or Hall of Mirrors, from older palaces of Delhi and Agra. Amber's Sheesh Mahal was perhaps influenced by the Mughals, but the sculptured elephants and peacocks are part of the Rajput tradition. They also borrowed from the Muslims the art of filigreeing

marble sandstone and introduced it in their palaces and *havelis* (traditionally designed houses). Jaipur is among the chief centres of stone carving in India, famous for its marble and sandstone work. The scarcity of timber and abundance of stone for building purposes made stonework a highly developed craft here.

Jali work, or fretwork, is supposed to have been the eastern artist's device to subdue the fierce heat of the sun while giving free access to the breeze. This delicate filigree is done on marble or sandstone, finely fretted into a network of geometrical combinations. *Jali* work was a Mughal innovation, first introduced into this country in Agra and Fatehpur Sikri. And though the Rajputs continued, as good Hindus, to cremate their dead, they are thought to have picked up from the Mughals the art of sepulchral adornment. Hence the cenotaphs on the outskirts of practically every city of Rajputana.

Above Amber is Jaigarh Fort. A vast treasure is supposed to have been buried in the fort but searches have never revealed any secret riches. On a clear day, Jaigarh Fort can be seen reflected in Amber's Maota Lake. Another stirring sight is that of Jaipur by night, seen from Nahargarh Fort which overlooks the city. Nahargarh can be clearly seen from Jaipur city, unlike Amber which is deeper in the mountains, or Jaigarh, which can only be seen from certain points. Nahargarh was built by Sawai Jai Singh II in 1734 as a resort for his wives. A gun used to be fired from atop the fort to mark the time according to the Jaipur solar observatory.

Jantar Mantar, the open air observatory behind the City Palace of Jaipur, is one of the unique contributions that Sawai Jai Singh II made to his people and to posterity. Like the other observatories built in Delhi, Mathura, Ujjain and Varanasi it has an equinoctial dial, the 'Samrat Yantra' or 'Supreme Instrument', to indicate the position of the sun and other heavenly bodies, and a variety of other instruments. It is the only stone observatory in the world, and its beautifully proportioned instruments are like fine pieces of sculpture. A keen astronomer, Sawai Jai Singh II delved deep into the subject and had the works of Euclid

A palace retainer at Jaipur's Chandra Mahal, part of the City Palace complex where the royal family resides. Loyalty dies hard, and old retainers still serve the family in a manner befitting royalty.
Facing page: *The Maharaja of Jaipur, Bhawani Singh, greets people on his birthday at his glittering City Palace. Though the titles are no longer officially recognised, several private celebrations of the former royal family continue to remain public events.*

Jaigarh, one of the three forts cresting the Aravalli capital of Jaipur, and once the repository of the great secret treasure of the royal family, also housed a gun foundry. It was here that this cannon, the Jaivana, was cast, believed to be the world's largest, though it has never had an occasion to be fired in defence.

and other scientists translated. Initially he built some metal instruments which can still be seen at the observatory. However, doubting their durability, he gave up metal masonry. An Arabic translation of Euclid's *Elements of Geometry* and a Sanskrit translation of Ptolemy called *Siddhanth Sar Kaustubh* are among the rare exhibits at the City Palace Museum.

Rajasthan abounds in forts and palaces and Jaipur is blessed with some of the finest. The City Palace was built by Sawai Jai Singh, though the later maharajas did make some additions. It is the most important palace in Jaipur, and after 1922 became the official seat of the Jaipur royal family. The former rulers still retain the seven-storeyed Chandra Mahal for their private use. The rest of this exotic palace is now a museum, known as the City Palace Museum. Its solid ivory and brass doors, its painted walls, the array of medieval armoury, its thrones, chandeliers, carpets, silver urns and art collection, all speak of the glorious past of the Rajput princes.

The Jagat Shiromani temple is dedicated to the memory of a prince who died young and is associated with the poet-saint Mira Bai. Stone elephants flank the carved gateway that forms its entrance.

The Hawa Mahal or 'Palace of the Winds', was a later addition to the palace complex, and was built in 1799 by Maharaja Sawai Pratap Singh. This unusual five-storeyed structure with its intricately wrought façade of casements tucked beneath arches and spires looms large over the bustling street below. No one quite knows why it was built, though it is said to have been dedicated to Lord Krishna by Pratap Singh who was a devotee of the Hindu god. It was probably used by aristocratic Rajput women to look out while they themselves remained unseen. Rajput women used to observe strict *purdah.*

There are many stories connected with the ubiquitous pink colouring of the city's buildings, but it is not known for certain when and why it was done. Some say that in the nineteenth century Maharaja Man Singh ordered the city's buildings to be painted a uniform pink to honour a visiting British dignitary. A more interesting explanation is that Sawai Jai Singh II was trying to build another Fatehpur Sikri (which is in red sandstone and white marble) without using either sandstone or marble.

Like its architecture, Jaipur's art is an achievement of the past. Devotion to Krishna is an important element in Rajput life. In the late eighteenth century, this was reflected in the intense Jaipur style of painting. In simple lines and pure colours, large, almost life-size pictures were painted, depicting the women of the court as Krishna's *gopis,* in the graceful movements of a dance. A somewhat diffused form of Mughal miniature style was also practised. As in the Mughal miniatures, court scenes and portraits, especially of the rulers, were most common. The Jaipur Museum has a good collection of these paintings.

Jaipur's crafts are, however, rich and living. An old resident has recorded elaborate notes on some of the crafts which flourished there and which assumed the proportions of an industry. One of these was the art of miniature painting, which was done on card, thick paper or gold-beater's skin. Large quantities of brightly coloured pictures of every grade of merit were produced throughout the state. For the best artists, it was an amazingly lucrative profession. In Jaipur, some of them were employed by the royal family, receiving salaries or land grants, with the privilege of working for private parties when not wanted in the palace. Where the son was gifted, these posts became hereditary.

Today, Jaipur is the gem and jewellery centre of northern India. A variety of precious stones which are cut and set in exquisite designs are available in the local market.

Jaipur is also famous for its enamel work. Mewar's silver mines feed jewellers' shops in Jaipur and Udaipur where this famous enamel work on silver, called *meenakari*, has its home. Said to have been introduced by Maharaja Man Singh I of Amber, this craft of colour engraving on gold, silver or copper has been perfected to a high art. Man Singh's gold and copper sceptre is said to have been the first of its kind. It is said to be the staff which the Maharaja bore when he stood before the throne of Emperor Akbar at the close of the sixteenth century. It was fifty-two inches long and composed of thirty-three cylinders of gold arranged on a central core of strong copper. Each of the gold cylinders was enamelled with figures of animals, landscapes and flowers.

Today, a variety of patterns are engraved on steel. The surface is burnished and then the colours are applied in the order of their fusibility. Those that can stand the greatest heat are applied first. When the colours are fixed, the steel is polished. All the colours of the rainbow can be applied on gold but only a few colours can be used with copper. *Meenakari* is found in many parts of India but Jaipur makes the best enamel jewellery.

Engraved brassware is another of Jaipur's metal crafts. Flowers, landscapes and jungle scenes are most common. These may be bold flowers or minute ones, designed on a lacquered surface.

The Mughal influence is still visible in Jaipur's marble and sandstone carvings and inlay work, and also in its carpets. The well known Jaipur carpets often have cypress and animal patterns against a dark red, blue or ivory coloured background with a floral border. The museum has an exotic collection of carpets.

The wealth of crafts in the city is indeed remarkable. *Bandhani* or tie-and-dye printing on fabric produces enchanting patterns. It is a popular art, said to be symbolic of maidenhood, love and marital happiness, and figures constantly in love lyrics and folk songs. Done on muslin, cotton or silk, it is widely used by women in both cities and villages as a *sari* or as a *dupatta* or veil which women drape over their embroidered skirts, called *ghagras*.

There are two methods of rendering tie-and-dye. In one, the draughtsman divides the whole surface of the cloth into one inch squares. It is then given to the knotter, usually a young girl, who picks up a little cloth at each corner of the squares and ties it into a knot with pack-thread, the number and position of the knots being decided by the pattern that the cloth has to take. With a

One of two silver urns on display at Jaipur's City Palace, recorded by the Guinness Book as the largest silver objects in the world. They were specially made for Madho Singh II, and used to carry Ganga water on his maiden journey to London to attend Edward VII's coronation. It was then believed that overseas travel sullied the pure.

The City Palace complex today houses a museum which displays the accoutrements of royalty and of the Kachwaha clan. The cream coloured palace in the background is the current residence of the former royals of the dynasty.

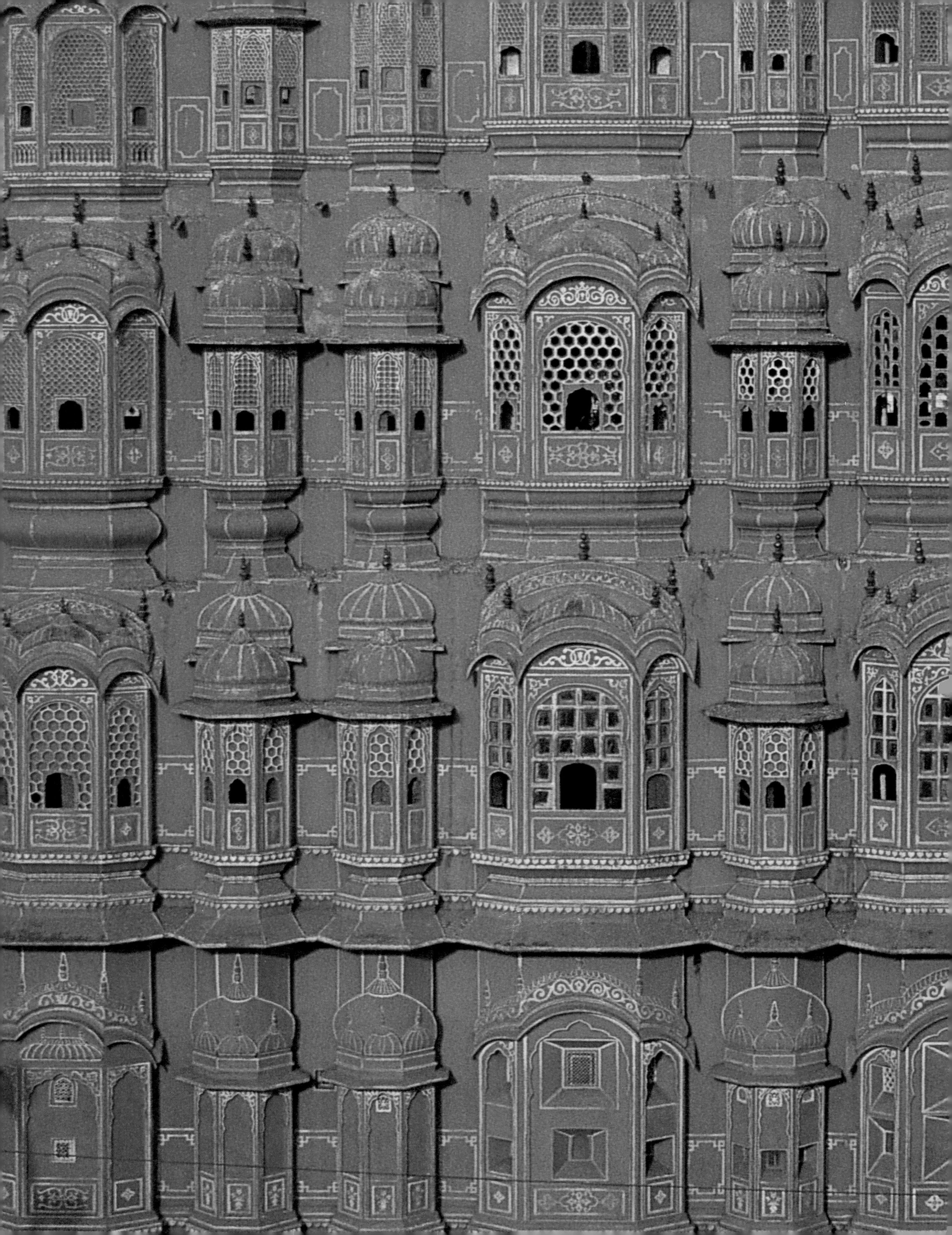

The Sheesh Mahal at Amber reflects the growing closeness of the house of Jaipur with the Mughals at Agra and Delhi. Mirrors would be imbedded into silver backdrops with translucent colours adding to the jewelled effect. ***Preceding pages 82-83:*** *A close-up of Hawa Mahal, Jaipur's signature building, with its 953 latticed windows built by Sawai Pratap Singh at the end of the 18th century and used by women of the zenana to watch street processions in privacy.*

different kind of knotting, a striped variation called *lahariya* (literally, 'ripples') is produced. The cloth is dyed in the chosen colour and the tied-up parts resist the dye. In the other method, the cloth is fastened onto a wooden block with pins set in the required design and the raised points are tied with waxed string.

To see craftsmen at work, another place to visit is Sanganer village, adjacent to the Jaipur airport. In Sanganer live and work the handblock printers whose delicate designs on cotton and calico have made the village famous in many parts of the world. The printers, who have practised this craft for over two centuries, used vegetable dyes in the past. Now chemical dyes are being used. Here men and women can be seen bending over the printing tables set up in the village houses or along the winding pathways. It is interesting that most of the Sanganer women prefer cheap synthetics to their beautiful hand printed *saris*. They say they are tired of looking at their own designs. Making hand made paper and printing on it is another Sanganer speciality. The main colour used here is an orange-red, with yellow and blue-black floral prints. Another small town called Bagru (also near Jaipur) has flooded the textile market, both domestic and overseas, with stunning circular designs printed on bed-spreads, table-cloths and clothes.

At Jaipur, one can also see the famous blue pottery of this region. This is notable more for the interplay of light and colour than for shapes. There are any number of blue pottery workshops. Jaipur pottery, like that of Delhi, is unusual in one respect. It is made of ground feldspar mixed with starch and gum and cannot be shaped on a wheel like clay but has to be moulded by hand. This is called *kamchini.* Of course, the traditional potter's wheel is also used for a different kind of product. The chief colours used are blue from the oxide of cobalt, green from the oxide of copper, and white. Some of the pottery is semi-translucent and in addition to blue and green, other combinations have now been evolved, such as canary yellow, dark blue and brown. Some of the best pieces are hand-painted with conventional floral or arabesque patterns.

Jaipur's footwear is also justly famed.

Atop Ganesh Pol is a network of galleries with pierced stone screens or jaalis that lent protection to the zenana women in purdah, while allowing them to observe events outside their apartments. Such screens also served a cooling purpose in the hot desert city. The characteristic floral paintings on polished plaster relief are particularly well developed here, and are a feature of many of Jaipur's palaces.

Its comfortable and informal slip-on shoes or *jooties* come in a variety of colours and designs. The sole is made of leather and the upper of leather covered with delicately embroidered cloth or velvet.

A minor craft in Jaipur is lac work. It is a delightful experience to watch lac bangles being made. The lac is melted in the customer's presence and shaped into bangles in the colours and designs chosen. The customer only has to wait for them to cool and they are ready to wear. They come in pink, red, yellow, green and black and are available in various shapes in simple or elaborate designs, in one colour or in a twirling combination.

Culturally, too, Jaipur is rich. Many of its past rulers, like the versatile Sawai Jai Singh II, were well versed in poetry and literature. Ram Singh II was proficient in Sanskrit, Hindi, English, Urdu and Rajasthani. Many famous Hindi poets flourished under the patronage of the Amber and Jaipur courts. Behari, the doyen of the *ritkalin*, or romantic school of Hindi poetry, was attached to the court of Jai Singh I. It is said he was paid one gold *mohur* (coin) for every *doha* or couplet he composed.

In the sixteenth century, the Krishna Bhakti Movement and Brajbhasha, the dialect of Hindi spoken around Mathura, spread to Amber. Two versions of the Rajasthani language developed. Pingal was the court language, popularized by Behari and used in poetry and romance. Dingal was the form in daily use and in the vigorous folklore. The purists considered Pingal (akin to Brajbhasha) a 'foreign language' inferior to the robust, virile and forceful Dingal which "comes to the ear like the sound of war drums and seems to sizzle like shifting sand dunes". Dingal songs are still sung in the villages. Today's poets use both Dingal and Pingal. Jaipur's proximity to Delhi and western Uttar Pradesh and its close contact with the Mughals have helped the spread of Khari Boli and Urdu as well.

Jaipur has also been an important centre of classicial music and dance. Many of India's top Kathak dancers are schooled in the Jaipur *gharana* or school, which lays a greater emphasis on footwork than the Lucknow *gharana*, evolved in a more fluid style.

The Jaipuri finds many occasions for gaiety and celebration. *Gangaur* is the women's festival when young girls and married women plant wheat and barley in earthen pots and pray to the Hindu goddess Gauri, or Parvati, the consort of Shiva, for a happy married life. This festival begins on the day after Holi and lasts eighteen days. Clay images of the deities are fashioned by deft fingers, dressed in rich clothes and ornaments and taken in a procession to be immersed in a tank. *Teej* is all fun, a festival of swings to celebrate the rainy season. There is another story connected with this festival, according to which *Teej*, too, is dedicated to Parvati, celebrating the day when she was reunited with Shiva after long "austerities". Girls and women take turns on gaily decorated swings, singing traditional songs as they swing to and fro. *Rakhi* is marked by women tying a decorative thread around their brothers' wrists to seek their protection.

Sheetla Mata, the powerful goddess who charms away smallpox, the brave Rani Sati of Jhunjhunu, the revered saint Ramdeo and Lord Mahavir, the twenty-fourth Jain Tirthankara, are a few of the innumerable deities and heroes worshipped. Like all Rajasthanis, the people of Jaipur love a festival or a fair. The grounds where the people camp to sell and buy camels, carts, cattle and goods are a sea of multi-coloured turbans— orange, yellow, red. The women wear gay *bandhani* skirts, veils and *saris*, and plenty of chunky silver jewellery. Bonfires are lit, and dances and music enliven the fair grounds.

Valour and sentiment, the mystic and the mundane—every desire, every mood and feeling finds expression in the Pink City.

PALACE HOTELS

IN 1947, THE PRINCELY STATES WERE merged into an independent, democratic India; a socialist government and populist movement placed curbs on the spendings and lifestyle of the princely order; among the casualties to this were their magnificent palaces which came under the land-ceiling act. They were taken over by the official machinery of the state to be turned into hospitals or schools or indifferent government offices, and only personal residences were retained by the royal families, though with funds ceasing, even these were difficult to maintain. In Jaipur, the royal family stayed at Rambagh Palace, the beautiful palace set in a garden and designed with every conceivable luxury of the age. Here, the handsome couple known in international circles as the Jaipurs, Maharaja Jai Singh II and his third bride, the vivacious Ayesha (or Gayatri Devi as she is better known) had thrown hundreds of parties, entertained members of the English and Indian aristocracy and made a home that featured in all the design magazines of the age. It was therefore, somewhat of a shock when in 1958 the maharaja decided that the best way to preserve the happy memories of the palace lay in converting it into a hotel.

In her autobiography, *A Princess Remembers*, she recalls: 'We were speech-

Top: *The City Palace complex includes the 18th century Jantar Mantar observatory of its founder-king. It is interesting to speculate on whether his love for astronomy arose from the the family's claimed ascent from the Sun God.*
Above: *Sisodia Rani ka Bagh, on the Agra road was built as a summer palace for an Udaipur princess.*
Facing page: *At the base of Amber and on the road to Jaipur, one comes across Jal Mahal, a former hunting lodge where the royal family would come to indulge its passion for shikar.*

A Jaipur citizen resplendent in his pink turban, relaxes in front of Amber's Ganesh Pol at the entrance to the private apartments facing the Diwan-i-Am, as he smokes a rolled-leaf cigarette known as a 'biri'.

less. Jai patiently went on explaining to us that times had changed and that it was no longer possible to keep Rambagh in the way it had always been, and deserved to be, maintained. If Rambagh had to be kept up in a proper way, it would have to be given up for a public cause. Jaipur badly needed a good hotel.'

In a way, that decision was to set the precedent to the city's several handsome palaces and mansions, converting it as it were into a city of palace hotels. To be in Jaipur and not to stay at a former royal residence appears almost a travesty, despite the capital's now several good, modern hotels.

The Rambagh still remains top-of-the-rung. This cream and white confection has a fairly simple, unadorned façade, with interiors that were best adapted to luxuriating in. Huge rooms, colonnaded corridors that double as deep verandahs, terraced gardens, a dining room with a sumptuously painted ceiling, a bar where a fountain is lined with the city's famous blue-pottery tiles, and rooms and suites with many of the original furnishings and objects make it a dream come alive for many vicarious, pleasure-seeking tourists. In the cold season, it is the base for several theme parties, and a startled visitor may find himself being greeted with rose-petals, scented *attar* and trumpeting elephants : not an unpleasant experience, and one that certainly brings alive princely India with all its glamorous ramifications.

Jai Mahal is different. Its impressive exterior is mostly modern, as are most of the rooms which, within, are disappointingly like those of most resort hotels. In a palace of a few rooms to a large hotel with many rooms, this was inevitable, but there is little about the façade thay betrays this union. The drive, the entrance and the public areas of the original palace have been retained, but the most wonderful aspect of this hotel is its garden. Laid when the newer portions of the palace were added, it recreates the first Mughal garden in India, at nearby Dholpur by the first of the great Mughal emperors, Babar. Its large driveway and extensive landscaping gives it a particular charm in desert country.

Of the royal residences, there is only

The entrance known as Ganesh Pol or Elephant Gate, so called because of the auspicious image of Ganesh painted 'araish' style above the doorway, led to the lavish Amber apartments. The rich paintings hint at some of the exotic architectural wealth that lay within.
Overleaf: *A dancer swirls to the rhythm of desert music in the richly painted Durbar Hall of Samode Palace. In such surroundings, it is easy to imagine the past with its evocative lifestyle. Samode Palace is currently one of the country's most popular palace hotels.*

one more, Rajmahal, that is being run as a hotel. This has few rooms, and the charm of an original palace, though it is inevitable that this too will soon become a larger, more updated palace hotel. Like Rambagh, this too has been home to the royal family, if only for a brief period.

The next in line, and closer in character to their original mood and atmosphere, are the homes of Jaipur's aristocracy. These, in the nature of country homes, are spacious personal residences that followed the royal example to become hotels, and have an appeal that is both personal and more directly charming. Take the case of Samode Haveli close to the entrance of the city. The actual seat of the family, at Samode, an hour's drive from Jaipur, is a wonderful retreat too, but their Jaipur mansion is far more exotic. Here are shaded courtyards and gardens, and as you climb the narrow steps to your rooms, you enter fantasyland. For most rooms have original paintings intact, splendidly executed, covering walls and ceilings, combined with turn-of-the-century furniture. As in most rambling homes, there is something new to discover at every bend: a painting or a photograph to be examined in greater detail; performers readying for an evening's entertainment; or perhaps just the aristocratic incumbents strolling casually through their family home as they go about their business.

Samode Haveli was built by Rawal Sheo Singh, a prime minister in the Jaipur court, who belonged to the Samode family that traces its lineage to Prithviraj Singh of Amber, the seventeenth prince in the house of the Kachwaha Rajputs. His father, Rawal Bairi Sal had wielded absolute power in court, and it was at this point in history that this line at the Chomu Nathawats made their money. The Samode family is known for its sensitivity to art and its patronage of the finest talent from the body of artisans then working in Jaipur. The result is two beautiful residences that are like art galleries, the workmanship equalling, if not superior to, Jaipur's City Palace. But it is Samode Palace, the fortfied residence outside Jaipur, once the seat of the Nathawat family, that comes closest to displaying the atmosphere of a medieval *thikana.* The road to Samode

Interior of Narain Niwas Palace : a handsome townhouse for the Kanota family that had its fortified settlement on Jaipur's outskirts, and has paid a rich contribution to the Jaipur royals in military service, it now runs its former homes as hotels.

village runs through an old gate, over cobbled roads on both sides of which are lined the houses of the people whose ancestors have contributed to Jaipur's martial history. Up, finally, to the grand sweep of steps that leads to the palace. Within, there are apartments touched with the shadows of the past, brilliant frescoes on the walls, the painted Sultan Mahal to relax in, and as a triumphal tour de force, the Durbar hall where in opulent surroundings, *mehfils* are recreated so that the chandelier-lit hall reverberates once again with music and laughter. It is hardly surprising that Samode Palace features so prominently in films and on television, the backdrop for Indian and international celluloid extravaganzas.

The former Shekhawati *thikana,* Bissau, too has a mansion in Jaipur being run as a hotel. The crowded approach to the building opens into a large garden, and steps lead up to the reception. Run by the family, as are most other *havelis* and mansions, the public areas are like a museum, complete with larger-than-life paintings, old photographs and silver jewellery placed amidst old books and artefacts. The rooms have a personalized, if inconsistent, charm, and much of the atmosphere originates from the affable, aristocratic owner and his genial wife.

Bissau's history, however, was not always 'soft'; its antecedents were of a rough clan reknowned for their prowess in the field. A story is told of a Bissau chieftain, Shyam Singh, in an Englishman's account who visited his court in 1808, thus: "At his palace I saw four Shekhawat chiefs and cousins — they were plain men, and seemed to be living in great harmony. While some of the others bore strong marks of the effect of opium especially noticeable in their eyes, one of them, Shyam Singh, seemed remarkably mild and well mannered but scarcely had I crossed the desert when I heard that Shyam Singh had murdered the three others at a feast, stabbing the first with his own hand". It was such *thakurs* who fought Jaipur's army till a British act forced them to acknowledge the Kachwahas as their rulers. It was then, too, that Jaipur's Bissau Palace was constructed, in 1919, under Thakur Rawal Raghubir

Rambagh palace exterior, with its sprawling lawns: once the centre of royal Jaipur, it was famous for parties thrown by the state's last rulers. Today Rambagh is a palace hotel.

Singh who has left behind his mark as a man of letters and of exquisite taste.

Another retreat, Narain Niwas, was actually a garden-residence for the Kanota family. With gardens and orchards laid around a modest house, it was only in this century that the most impressive parts of this mansion were laid and decorated with wall paintings in the trompe l'oeil style. In between the painted pillars are paintings of past members of the family, and retainers in uniform glide through these halls of history in hushed silence. Popular as a hotel with European tourists, Narain Niwas makes up with its quaint charm what is lacks in comfort, though its spacious rooms alone would put most other hotels to shame.

The Kanota family hails from Jodhpur, and in the 19th century found employment as senior officers in the Jaipur army before being given *jagirs* (a titular land holding) in 1872. Close, personal allies of the Jaipur maharaja, it was Thakur Narayan Singh who built the outhouse where the current Narain Niwas stands. His heir, the famous General Amar Singh whose diaries tell much of international events of that age, laid the foundation for the mansion in 1927, completing the building in 1932. The current incumbent converted it into a hotel in 1978. The *thikana* itself, a half hour's drive from Jaipur, has a small fort within which the family palace too is a hotel.

Mandawa House, Khetri House and Shahpura House too symbolize a way of living that is of the past, each stressing almost individually on an atmosphere that has been retained in the mid-19th to early-20th centuries.

This again is best symbolized in Jamwa Ramgarh, the hill-encircled lake resort that was once the hunting ground for the Jaipur royals. Here, Ramgarh Lodge, the former hunting retreat too has been converted into a small hotel. The mood is magnificent. The hall and corridors are lined with shooting trophies, the rooms feature the original furniture and paintings, the lights that hang from the ceiling are those that were first suspended here early in the century.

Palace living in Jaipur is a way of life, and something every visitor to the city should experience, if only to re-live for a few hours, the splendour of princely India.

On The High Road

THE 'GOLDEN TRIANGLE' LENDS itself most to surface travel, and the highway option may prove the best for there is so much more to see and do, that the journey itself appears more important than arrival at one of the pivotal destinations.

Delhi-Jaipur Highway

With Delhi as the stepping-off point, it is best to take the 265-km high road to Jaipur. The topography changes rapidly, from the bustling city with its leafy avenues to the suburbs around the airport (the landing of flights, as you careen down the road, is a memorable experience), to the highway skirting alongside or boldly through little village settlements. If you're the kind who likes to stop frequently, there's a large number of restaurants, motels and wayside inns for rest-and-refreshment, beginning with the well-landscaped Jungle Babbler complex at Dharuhera, barely an hour out of Delhi. The midway point is Behror, with catering and bar facilities.

However, for an experience that's radically different, almost midway, and just into Rajasthan, is the erstwhile fortress of Neemrana. This 15th century fortified palace belonged to the local chieftain, and has been in the family till recently, absorbing Rajput, Jat and Mughal influences through the centuries in its architecture, and ending up with a touch of British severity. Dwindling fortunes led the chieftain to abandon his home, till it found new ownership among art-restorers who have lovingly patched it up again, so that the fortress is now an experience-hotel. The grand rooms have now been re-designated and the spaces imaginatively turned around, yet without losing sight of the feeling of history which breathes so easily over its walls. In fact, the interplay of spaces has lent it a creativity which was a hallmark of the old palaces within the region, for successive rulers were always adding their own apartments to their palaces, while redesignating the use of old ones.

Neemrana deserves more than just a sally through its gates, and a sightseeing tour. The fingers of the sun god caressing its glowing walls in the early morning, while the cool desert wind plays a requiem to a lost empire; the blazing noon sky when you relax indoors with the finest cuisine to be found along the highway; and finally, the flaming orange of sunset which recreates a *son et lumiere* even as evening shadows and the sound of music and dance invoke the past not in the pages of a history book but in a home that has been alive for five centuries.

Just beyond Delhi, near the Gurgaon crossing, if you were to take a wrong turn, you would still not go off track for it would only be an alternate, less-busy, slightly longer route to Jaipur. Of course, if you're deliberatly taking this route, chances are you're thinking of spending time at Sariska, the tiger reserve which is midway along this highway.

Sariska was a private hunting reserve for the rulers of Alwar, and after independence was turned into a protected national park. More recently, with the launch of Project Tiger to offer special protection to this endangered, Indian species, it was declared a tiger reserve. However, it is difficult to spot tiger here for the hills and valleys are heavily forested, and the absence of flat plains makes it almost impossible to come across this feline species without appointment! Much more easy to spot, on just a casual ride through the sanctuary, are deer, langur, even jungle cat, and a rich avifaunal wealth.

At Sariska, again, one has the choice of staying in the erstwhile hunting lodge (a modest description for this palace) with its extensive lawns. The maharajas camped here when on shoots, and royals from other states, countries and viceroys have been entertained here. The tradition of hospitality now continues, even though the only shooting permissible is through camera lenses.

The route via Sariska also allows one the opportunity of visiting Alwar, an erstwhile princely kingdom that is now a provincial town with its bazaars and busy chowks bustling with a variety of motorised and animal-drawn traffic. The museum and the palaces are a magnificent heritage left behind by the royal family, though most of the latter remain closed to the public. A little distance from here is a lakeside retreat, that of Siliserh, where the royals would come for duck shoots, and to luxuriate at this pleasure palace. For overlooking a sharp rocky overhang over the lakes is this miniature palace: this is how Rapunzel's castle must have looked, and if you wish to participate in this fairy tale, all you have to do is check-in, for it is being run as a hotel by the state tourism corporation.

No matter which of the two alternate routes you choose, the two meet up well before Jaipur, passing through the town of Shahpura, a part of the Shekhawati region of Rajasthan where a scion of the family whose ancestor gave the region its name, still resides, and whose home too is now a heritage hotel. A detour on the road takes you to Samode, the *thikana* of a powerful family that influenced the affairs of Jaipur and where the erstwhile palace is now a highly successful period hotel. Further along the highway, where the road turns towards Amber, a short detour will get you to Ramgarh, a large natural lake eyelashed by forested hills. This too was a hunting lodge that is now a hotel, its interiors replete with trophies from successful shoots, and the large rooms still done up in furniture once used by the family.

Jaipur-Agra Highway

With so much on the Delhi-Jaipur highway, the Jaipur-Agra road seems almost empty in comparison. Stepping out of Jaipur, past the garden retreats of Vidyadharji ka Bagh and Sisodiya Rani ka Bagh, is the Agra route, almost immediately thereafter stumbling through the former *thikanas* of Kanota (within twin battlements, this castle-retreat is now a hotel, but you need to book in advance) and Nayala (a private hotel resort still not developed for public use). There's a midway point for a break, the road runs along Fatehpur with its magnificient stone carvers, but the next major halt is Bharatpur, the country's best known and largest sanctuary for birds, and a national park with deer, python and other species to be spotted.

Bharatpur reserve was artificially developed by the rulers of Bharatpur state for duck shoots, after laying a complex network of aqueducts. It has a very large variety of indigenous waterbirds and winter migrants, the Siberian crane among the latter. The roads of the sanctuary are best discovered on bicycle (available on hire), as birdsong fills the morning air, and lends it a reverential tone at vesper hour.

Bharatpur was a powerful Jat kingdom that was once successful in laying seige upon Delhi, capturing the throne for a brief moment of glory in history; it was often in conflict with both its powerful neighbours, Agra and Jaipur. The fort of the Jat kingdom is open to public, its spatial apartments almost enveloped by the sprawling tentacles of public administration, education, bazaars and private residences. The turn of the century Golbagh palace is now strictly a private residence, though a portion of the building is being renovated as a hotel.

The apogee of Jat architecture is Deeg, the nearby retreat where the Bharatpur rulers would summer in the more tranquil environs of a dream city they laid with meticulous detail. The characteristic roofs, the gardens with their coloured fountains, the pavilions which would simulate the conditions of the Indian monsoon to bring cooling relief, war booty from Maratha and Mughal campaigns, the large lounges, and the wonderful Indian dining hall with its low horse-shoe shaped marble table, are some of the highlights of this city, now peopled with tourists, but once the envy of its powerful neighbours, and of the British imperial power.

Agra-Delhi Highway

Agra to Delhi, the highway skirts Krishna-country, Mathura and Vrindaban. This is where the boy-god spent his youth, stealing milk and butter from earthen pitchers where it would be stored, and getting into a number of mischevious pranks which have gone on to popularise him in the lore of the region. Mathura was the capital of the Kushan empire from the 1st to the 3rd century, and was visited by international travellers from the Chinese Fa-hien and Huen-Tsiang to the Italian Tavernier, till an Afghan invader, Muhammad Ghuri, plundered the city in the 11th century, leaving it bereft; it was sacked twice in the 18th century, nothing remaining of 'one of the most sumptuous edifices in all India'. Today, it is best known for its association with Krishna, and a number of temples and *ashrams* testify to that belief.

Mathura forms a part of the region of Brajbhumi which encompasses an area that is 70 km long and 45 km wide, and stretches across both banks of the Yamuna. While Mathura was both capital and a town of no mean significance, Vrindaban (literally, a forest of basil plants) remained a forest-retreat and settlement. As before, the *ghats* along the banks of the Yamuna where the devout come for purifying baths, forms the focus of attention at Vrindaban.

While both continue to be acknowledged for their religious association and their festivities (Holi in Mathura is particularly well known), it is well worth visiting Mathura for its Museum which has an outstanding collection, mainly of sculptural art, spanning two thousand years of history. This ranges from a 4th century BC mother goddess to the moulded clay sculptures of the Sunga dynasty (2nd - 1st century BC) to the sandstone techniques of the Kushan dynasty when Buddhist and Jain art dominated the region, leading to the Gupta period with its golden age, and finally giving way to a more formal approach in the medieval ages of Hindu art.

The sculptural art of Mathura is important for two reasons : it first gave form to the Buddha, till then only symbolic; and it combined local influence with Indo-Bactrian and Iranian traditions to create a visual form that was pleasing and is recognised for its excellence all over the country.

*Royal retreats of the Alwar princes, Siliserh (**opposite page**) is like Rapunzel's castle while Sariska Palace (**above**) sprawls in luxurious comfort. Both are currently hotels.*
Overleaf: *Holi being celebrated in Vrindaban: special festivities mark the event in this region, for its close association with Krishna and the milkmaids have given it a fairytale charm.*